AAT

TECHNICIAN
NVQ AND DIPLOMA PATHWAY (DIPLOMA)

REVISION COMPANION   Unit 17

Implementing Audit
Procedures

BPP
LEARNING MEDIA

Fourth edition April 2008
First edition 2004

ISBN 9780 7517 4637 2 (previous edition 9780 7517 3233 0)

British Library Cataloguing-in-Publication Data
A catalogue record for this book is available from the British Library

Published by

BPP Learning Media Ltd
BPP House
Aldine Place
London
W12 8AA

www.bpp.com/learningmedia

Printed in Great Britain by Martins the Printers, Berwick-upon-Tweed

Your learning materials, published by BPP Learning Media Ltd, are printed on paper sourced from sustainable, managed forests.

We are grateful to the AAT for permission to reproduce specimen assessments. All answers have been prepared by BPP Learning Media Ltd.

CONTENTS

INTRODUCTION

This is BPP Learning Media's AAT Revision Companion for Unit 17, Implementing Audit Procedures. It is part of an integrated package of AAT materials.

It has been written in conjunction with the BPP Course Companion, and has been carefully designed to enable students to practise all aspects of the requirements of the Standards of Competence and performance criteria. It is fully up to date as at April 2008 and reflects the revised Standards of Competence.

This Revision Companion contains these key features:

- graded activities corresponding to each chapter of the Course Companion
- a practice skills test
- the AAT's specimen skills test

The emphasis in all activities and questions is on the practical application of the skills acquired. All activities, practice assessments and simulations have full answers prepared by BPP Learning Media Ltd.

Tutors adopting our Companions (minimum of ten Course Companions and ten Revision Companions per Unit, or ten Combined Companions as appropriate) are entitled to free access to the Lecturers' Area resources, including the Tutor Companion. To obtain your log-in, e-mail lecturersvc@bpp.com.

Home Study students are also entitled to access to additional resources. You will have received your log-in details on registration.

If you have any comments about this book, please e-mail helendarch@bpp.com or write to Helen Darch, AAT Publishing Manager, BPP Learning Media Ltd, BPP House, Aldine Place, London W12 8AA.

Using this Revision Companion

You should work through the practice activities methodically chapter by chapter. This is because some of the questions follow the course of two audits (Glad Rags Limited and Greenfingers Limited) and the answer to an earlier question may be relevant to the answer to a later question.

Diploma Pathway

This Revision Companion can be used by all AAT students, whether following the NVQ route or the Diploma Pathway to the AAT qualification.

chapter 1:
THE BUSINESS ENVIRONMENT

1   What records must be kept by a business entity once it has registered as a company?

2   Registered companies must have an audit. What is an audit and who is exempt from the requirement to have an audit?

chapter 2:
INTRODUCTION TO AUDIT

1   Explain what is meant by external audit and internal audit, highlighting the difference between the two.

2   For the last few years your firm has helped Celina, a sole trader, prepare her accounts for HM Revenue and Customs. Celina is about to incorporate her business and has asked your advice on the advantages to the company of having its accounts audited (you may assume that the company would be able to claim exemption from audit). Advise Celina.

3   What is the difference between an auditor's legal relationship with the company being audited and other interested third parties (stakeholders)?

4   What is the Auditing Practices Board and what relevance does it have to UK auditors?

5   You have started work for a company that is in the process of being audited for the first time. The directors have heard that the auditors do not certify that the accounts are correct but instead speak of obtaining reasonable assurance and eventually expressing an opinion on the truth and fairness of the accounts. Explain to the directors the basis on which auditors develop their audit opinion on accounts.

6   You are the audit senior on the audit of Glad Rags Limited, which will be commencing shortly. Your audit assistant is Jules Devoran, who is new to the firm and has little experience of auditing. The audit manager has therefore asked that you explain some fundamental aspects of auditing to him.

Compile brief notes for Jules' benefit explaining the following matters:

- Working papers and what they should contain
- The difference between a permanent audit file and a current audit file
- An audit engagement letter

7   The owner of Glad Rags Limited has discussed with the audit partner the possibility that she will seek to sell the business in the near future. No one else at the company is aware of her plans.

For Jules' benefit, set out the auditors' duty of confidentiality, and how you and Jules should treat this piece of information when you attend the client to conduct the audit.

8   You are the auditor of a premiership football club of which you are also a fan. You have applied for a season ticket but there is a three year waiting list.

One of the directors suggests that he can help you to jump the queue and if you make out a cheque for the season ticket, he will sort out a seat for you in the directors' box in time for the next home game. How should you react and why?

> **Background information – Greenfingers Limited**
>
> Greenfingers Limited is a long-standing client of the audit firm. It is a gardening retail operation which has three retail outlets, the biggest of which also has a small café on the premises. The shops purchase plants from nurseries and other gardening companies and have a number of 'hardware' suppliers, who supply pots and fences and other non-plant stock. The shops are open seven days a week except for Christmas and Boxing days.

9   You have been selected as audit senior on the audit of Greenfingers Limited. You are at the client's premises with your audit junior, Clare Purdey, carrying out a pre-planning visit. You have been given a small office to work in and have been provided with a key to that office.

You have just returned to the office having been speaking to the accountant of Greenfingers Limited. You have found that Clare is not in the office and the door is unlocked. The prior year audit files are open on the table of the office.

Outline why this is bad audit practice and what Clare ought to have done in this situation.

10   During the course of your pre-planning work you discover that the managing director for many years, David Green, is retiring in March, prior to the audit beginning. He is being succeeded as managing director by his son, Peter Green, the only other working director, who has had little involvement with the auditors as he has previously worked more in operations.

Explain whether this information will have any impact on your pre-audit work.

11   Your firm of Accountants, in common with many other firms of accountants and auditors, issues to its staff an audit manual which contains, amongst other matters, recommended procedures to be adopted in carrying out audits. A number of these recommended procedures relate to physical observation of stock counts (inventory counts) and review of stocktaking (inventory count) instructions which is also recommended by auditing standards.

Owing to pressure of work, you neglected to arrange for the physical observation of stocks (inventory) at the premises of Leesmoor Ltd at 31 March 20X4, but your review of stocktaking instructions indicated that company procedures appeared to be in order. You decided to accept the amount at which stock was stated in the financial statements at 31 March 20X4 on the grounds that:

(a)   The stocktaking instructions appeared to be satisfactory
(b)   No problems had arisen in determining physical stock quantities in previous years, and
(c)   The figures in the financial statements generally 'made sense'.

You issued your unqualified audit report on 28 May 20X4 and unbeknown to you Leesmoor used the financial statements and the audit report for the purpose of obtaining material additional finance from a third party in the form of an unsecured long-term loan. Unfortunately, in October 20X4 the company ran into financial difficulties and was forced into liquidation as a result of which the long-term loan holder lost the amount of his loan. During the liquidation proceedings it became clear that stock quantities at 31 March 20X4 had been considerably overstated.

Task

Explain the probable legal position of your firm in respect of the above matter commenting specifically on the following:

(a)   The possibility of demonstrating your firm were negligent

(b)   The fact that the stocks figure in the financial statements apparently 'made sense'

(c)   The fact that you were not informed that the financial statements and your audit report were to be used to obtain additional finance.

6

chapter 3:
THE COMPANY ENVIRONMENT (CONTROLS)

1   What are the five components of an internal control system?

2   What is a control environment? How do directors affect the control environment?

3   What is an information system, and what is the difference between a manual and a computerised system?

4   Explain what control activities are, giving 4 examples of general types of control activity.

5   What risks to a company might exist in extending credit to its customers, and what control activities can be put in place to mitigate the risks?

6   What risks to a company might exist in despatching goods and invoicing, and what control activities can be put in place to mitigate the risks?

7   You have now begun the audit of Glad Rags Limited. Review the information given about the purchases and creditors system given below and identify the controls that are present.

Accounting systems information – Glad Rags Limited

Purchases

The company keeps basic stocks of all the fabric and threads required to manufacture goods from their catalogue. When stocks are fall to a certain level, the stores manager requisitions a pre-set amount of that stock. There are certain fabrics that are only used for a limited number of stocks. That fabric will only be re-ordered if a sales order is placed for items requiring the fabric.

When the purchases department receive a requisition, they place the order with the approved supplier at a prearranged price. An order document is written out and kept in the orders pending file.

When the fabric or thread is received, the stores manager ensures that the quality is suitable and checks the goods against the order. The order is then passed to the accounts department and placed in the pending invoices file.

When the invoice is received, the accounts assistant, Beth Simpkins, checks the invoices against the order to ensure the price and quantity are correct and checks the VAT has been calculated correctly. She initials the invoices to show that these checks have been carried out and gives the invoice a sequence number. The invoice is then entered into the purchase ledger on the computer.

> Beth prepares cheques for payment at the end of each two weeks and passes them to the director, Gladys Barton, for signature and approval. The invoices are included with the cheques as evidence of the debt.
>
> Most suppliers send statements at the end of the month which Beth reconciles to the purchase ledger balances. The purchase ledger control account is agreed to the total of the purchase ledger balances at the end of the month.

8   Using the accounting system information given below, identify controls present in the payroll system at Glad Rags.

> **Accounting systems information**
>
> *Payroll*
>
> There are two payrolls, which are computerised and prepared by the director, Gladys Barton. Machining staff are paid by piece which is recorded and approved by the factory overseer, Peter Benning. Machining staff are paid weekly. Office and other administrative staff are paid a standard salary on a monthly basis.
>
> The weekly payroll produces an exception report if machining staff are paid more than 20% more than their weekly average over the year. This exception report is checked back to the piece sheets prepared and approved by Peter Benning. Machinists are paid in cash which must be collected personally and signed for by the employee.
>
> Monthly payments are made by automatic bank transfer from Glad Rags' bank account to the employees' bank account.

9   During your visit to Greenfingers Limited you are assessing the systems of the company. The company makes no sales on credit, so in previous years the audit firm has made several recommendations concerning sales controls operating in the business to reduce the risk to the business and the audit of cash sales.

Using the accounting systems information below, identify controls present in the sales system.

> **Accounting systems information – sales**
>
> Sales are carried out at the tills in each of the shops. Cashiers have individual passwords to access the tills and must log out of the till when they are no longer using it. However, staff passwords are widely known and may not only be used by the relevant individual. Tills not in use are locked shut.
>
> All stock is marked with prices and a stock type code (for example, plants), both of which are entered into the till. Till rolls are retained for each day and sales totals from the till rolls are entered into sales ledgers. The till rolls are retained for the auditors. The tills are emptied early in the morning before the shops open by the cashiers and the contents are counted up and then (except for a £50 float for each till) taken to the accounts department by a staff member, where the till rolls are reconciled to the cash and credit slips and entered into the sales ledger. The cash is then banked. The cash counting is supposed to commence at 8am and be

completed by the time the shop opens at 9am, at which time the doors to the shops are unlocked. However, the cash count is often commenced late.

The café also has a till and operates in a similar way, except that no stock code is required, given that all the café takings are logged as café takings.

10 Topbooks Ltd is a medium sized company with a mainframe computerised accounting system. The company's computer department operates the mainframe computer and a batch processing system is in use. A chief accountant is in charge of the accounts department and there is a sufficient number of employees to ensure adequate segregation of duties throughout the accounting system.

Owing to the diverse range of book titles available and the number of publishers, Topbooks Ltd has over 2,000 supplier accounts in its purchase ledger (payables ledger).

As the audit senior for the audit of the company's accounts you are now evaluating the controls maintained over the accounting system.

Task

You are required to brief the audit junior on the following issues:

(a) Explain the purpose of using batch control totals in a computerised accounting system and identify three control totals that may be used when processing purchasing data from purchase invoices. Give an example of each control total identified.

(b) List and explain the purpose of five programmed controls that you would expect to find over the processing of data through the computerised purchases system of Topbooks Ltd.

(c) Describe five controls that should be exercised over the suppliers' details standing data files in the company's purchase ledger (payables ledger) system, and for each one of these controls describe an appropriate test of controls that you would wish to carry out.

chapter 4:
AUDITING SYSTEMS

1   What methods may auditors use to record company systems?

2   What is a walkthrough test?

3   What two approaches could auditors take to an audit as a result of their assessment of control risk?

4   When are auditors likely to test controls, assuming that they have decided to do so?

5   Use the accounting system information for sales at Glad Rags Limited given below to complete the internal control questionnaire also given below.

Accounting system information

Sales

The company manufactures clothes to order from a catalogue.

When an order is received, the sales department checks that the customer has not exceeded their credit limit and then issues a two-part order document. The sales department fill in the appropriate values for the order. One copy is sent to the production department in order for the order to be completed and the other is filed alphabetically in the customer file in the sales department.

Once the order is completed, two-part despatch notes are raised. When the factory manager, Ian Jones, has checked the order, one copy of the despatch note is despatched with the goods (to be signed and returned), and one part is matched to the production department's sales order and sent to accounts to raise the invoice. Jane Hill raises the invoices from the order and despatch note, enters them on the computer and sends them out to customers.

Most customers pay in around 60 days. Cheques are passed to Beth Simpkins, one of the accounts assistants, when they come in and she updates the cashbook and the sales ledger. Cheques are banked twice a week. Cheques are kept securely in the safe until banking.

Jane sends out statements to customers each month. Glad Rags' customers are mostly all reputable high street stores and there are rarely bad debts.

Internal control questionnaire – sales and debtors system

Question	Yes/No	Comment
Are orders only accepted from low credit risks?	Y	
Are despatches checked by appropriate personnel?	Y	
Are goods sent out recorded?	Y	
Are customers required to give evidence of receipt of goods?		
Are invoices checked to despatch notes and invoices?		
Are invoices prepared using authorised prices?		
Are invoices checked to ensure they add up correctly?		
Are sales receipts matched with invoices?		
Are statements sent out regularly?		
Are overdue accounts reviewed regularly?		
Are there safeguards over post received to ensure that cheques are not intercepted?		
Are bankings made daily?		
Would it be appropriate to perform tests of control in this area? (Give reason/reasons in the comments box.)		

6   Set out two weaknesses in the accounting system for sales at Glad Rags Limited to be included in a report to the directors. You should also set out the possible consequence of each weakness and your recommendation for improvement.

7   Using the accounting system for purchases below and your identification of the controls in it from the previous chapter, note the tests of controls that could be performed to confirm the application of those controls at Glad Rags Limited.

Accounting systems information

Purchases

The company keeps basic stocks of all the fabric and threads required to manufacture goods from their catalogue. When stocks are fall to a certain level, the stores manager requisitions a pre-set amount of that stock. There are certain fabrics that are only used for a limited number of stocks. That fabric will only be re-ordered if a sales order is placed for items requiring the fabric.

When the purchases department receive a requisition, they place the order with the approved supplier at a prearranged price. An order document is written out and kept in the orders pending file.

When the fabric or thread is received, the stores manager ensures that the quality is suitable and checks the goods against the order. The order is then passed to the accounts department and placed in the pending invoices file.

When the invoices is received, the accounts assistant, Beth Simpkins, checks the invoices against the order to ensure the price and quantity are correct and checks the VAT has been calculated correctly. She initials the invoices to show that these checks have been carried out and gives the invoice a sequence number. The invoice is then entered into the purchase ledger on the computer.

Beth prepares cheques for payment at the end of each two weeks and passes them to the director, Gladys Barton, for signature and approval. The invoices are included with the cheques as evidence of the debt.

Most suppliers send statements at the end of the month which Beth reconciles to the purchase ledger balances. The purchase ledger control account is agreed to the total of the purchase ledger balances at the end of the month.

8   Using the accounting system for wages below and your identification of the controls in it from the previous chapter, state four tests of control over Glad Rags' payroll system, stating the control objective and the control that you are testing.

Accounting systems information

Payroll

There are two payrolls, which are computerised and prepared by the director, Gladys Barton. Machining staff are paid by piece which is recorded and approved by the factory overseer, Peter Benning. Machining staff are paid weekly. Office and other administrative staff are paid a standard salary on a monthly basis.

The weekly payroll produces an exception report if machining staff are paid more than 20% more than their average for the year. This exception report is checked back to the piece sheets prepared and approved by Peter Benning. Machinists are paid in cash which must be collected personally and signed for by the employee.

Monthly payments are made by automatic bank transfer from Glad Rags' bank account to the employees' bank account.

9   Using the accounting system information given in the questions relating to Chapter 3, identify two weaknesses in the sales system at Greenfingers Limited that could be included within a management letter, pointing out the weakness, its consequence and a recommendation to improve the system.

10 You are the audit senior reviewing the operation of the purchase system of Woodright Ltd, and are trying to decide whether you can rely on the system for the purpose of your audit. Read the details of the purchase system set out below before attempting the tasks for this question.

Task 1

(a) List the potential misstatement or problems that could arise in a system such as Woodright's.

(b) Write down a matching list stating which controls exist in the Woodright system to prevent these potential misstatement or problems occurring.

(c) Identify the control objective satisfied from the following list. All transactions are:

 (i) Recorded
 (ii) Valid
 (iii) Properly valued
 (iv) Reflected in proper accounting period
 (v) Correctly classified
 (vi) Correctly posted

Present your answer to parts (a) to (c) in a table, matching potential misstatements with controls and control objectives.

Task 2

State whether you feel that you will be able to rely on the purchases system of Woodright Ltd.

PURCHASES SYSTEM

Requisition

The originator (whoever needs the purchase) fills in a Purchase Requisition Note (PRN). The PRN is sent to Mrs Clementine in the Buying Department. She approves the order and finds an appropriate supplier. The Buying Department Supervisor, Amanda Costa, makes up a 4-part Purchase Order (PO) from the PRN and the supplier's standard price list as follows.

Copy 1 – White – to supplier
Copy 2 – Blue – filed in numerical order, matched with PRN
Copy 3 – Green – filed in alphabetical order by supplier
Copy 4 – Pink – sent to Mr Ho (Stores)

Every week, Amanda Costa reviews the alphabetical file of POs to check for unfilled orders. If necessary, suppliers are contacted.

Goods arrival

When they arrive at the warehouse, goods are counted and checked for quantity against the PO. Mr Ho then completes a 3-part pre-numbered Goods Received Note (GRN) as follows.

Details of missing or damaged goods are entered.

(a) If delivery quantity = PO quantity, then the 'order completed' box on the GRN is ticked. In the case of partial delivery this box is left blank.

(b) The GRN is signed by the counter and by Mr Ho.

Copy 1 – White – matched with PO by Mr Ho, filed numerically
Copy 2 – Blue – sent to Buying Dept
Copy 3 – Green – sent to Ms Poulos (also in Stores)

Ms Poulos updates the stock (inventory) records, and then files the GRNs in date order.

Every quarter, cyclical stock counts (inventory counts) are carried out; recorded quantities are compared to actual amounts; variances are reported and explained; and the stock (inventory) records are updated as required.

Buying Department

Amanda Costa compares the GRN (Copy 2, Blue) to the PO (Copy 3, Green) and the goods received are ticked off on the PO. Then either of the following takes place.

(a) Order completed

The matched GRN and PO are sent to Accounts to Mr Bobat (Accounts Payable Supervisor).

(b) Order not yet complete

Photocopy taken of PO, Copy 3, green. The original is matched to the GRN and sent to Mr Bobat. The photocopy is returned to the alphabetical file.

Accounts Department

Mr Bobat and Miss Stuart (Accounts Payable Clerk) receive invoices from suppliers. These are stamped with a grid stamp and numbered sequentially.

The invoices are matched with the GRN/PO; arithmetically checked, and the grid stamp is then initialled and the invoices are then sent to the accountant, Miss Madigan. All unmatched GRN/POs are reviewed weekly.

Miss Madigan authorises the invoice for payment and puts the Nominal Ledger (NL) Code on the grid stamp.

Where goods are missing or have been damaged, a 3-part Debit Note (DN) is made up as follows.

Copy 1 – White – to supplier
Copy 2 – Blue – sent with GRN/PO/invoice to Accounts Payable
Copy 3 – Green – filed in numerical order

The DNs are separated in Accounts Payable and filed alphabetically. When a Credit Notes (CN) is received from a supplier, it is grid-stamped and the arithmetic is checked. The CN is then matched to its related DN and processed in batches in the same way as invoices (see below). The file of unmatched debit notes is reviewed weekly.

Invoices are collected into batches in Accounts Payable as they are returned from the accountant. The batch total (invoice value) is recorded on a Batch Header Slip (BHS) and entered in a batch book.

The batches of invoices and credit notes are sent to a computer bureau for processing. The bureau updates the Purchase Ledger (Payables Ledger) (PL) and produces a Purchase Invoice Listing (Payables Invoice listing) (PIL).

The total on the PIL is agreed to the BHS (initialled by Miss Stuart) and to the batch book. The batch book is reviewed weekly by Mr Bobat to ensure that all batches have been returned by the bureau.

The PILs are filed in date order.

Month-end procedures

At the end of the month, the computer bureau produces a Purchase Ledger Listing (PLL). Mr Bobat reconciles all the major supplier statements for the month to the PLL and produces a Purchase Ledger control account reconciliation. The reconciliation is reviewed by Miss Madigan. The PLLs are filed in date order; the suppliers' statements are filed in alphabetical order. The Nominal Ledger is updated by Miss Madigan in a journal at the end of the month.

11   Still working on the audit of Woodright Ltd, you decide to test controls over purchases. The first test you perform is as follows.

Select a sample of 10 invoices from the purchase ledger and:

(a)   Ensure the invoice has been initialled as evidence of matching to GRN and of authorisation.
(b)   Re-perform matching invoice to GRN.

The documents that relate to the sample that you have selected are given on the following pages.

Task

Perform the test and document the work done. Your working papers should give the test objective, the work done, the results and the conclusions drawn. You should also show the invoices tested, giving the invoice number, date, supplier, goods and Goods Received Note number. You should indicate what tests have been performed on each invoice.

PURCHASE INVOICES

VAT No. 3 719 846 6

Green Forest Timber

Accounts receivable
48, Dunstable Rd
Newmarket
0312 489 273

Woodright Ltd
324 Daisy Road
Birmingham
B1 4LJ

INVOICE NUMBER

113479116

Date	Account no.	Transport	Terms
31.01.X3	W007		30 DAYS NET

Description	Amount
500m 6cm pine planking	2,500.00
Vat @17.5%	437.50
Amount due	2,937.50

RECEIVED

Inv No.	100948
Date	1/2/X3
Calcs (sign)	RS
Auth (sign)	PJM
NL Code	170 £2.500.00 900 £437.50

Reg office 48, Dunstable Rd, Newmarket Reg No 113459118

17

POTS OF PAINT LTD

The Paint Co Ltd
Unit 5
Farsight Estate
Newcastle upon Tyne
NT4 1SP
091 317 449

INVOICE NO	S453/91684	
INVOICE DATE	26/02/X3	
ACCOUNT NO	12374	
DELIVER TO:	Inv add.	
OUR ORDER NO	5011487	
YOUR ORDER NO	PO4381	

RECEIVED

Inv No.	101896
Date	28/2/X3
Calcs (sign)	RS
Auth (sign)	PJM
NL Code	472 £2610.00
	900 £456.75

SALES INVOICE

INVOICE TO:

WOODRIGHT LTD
324 DAISY RD
BIRMINGHAM
B1 4LJ

PRODUCT	DESCRIPTION / SERIAL NOS	QTY	LIST PRICE	NETT PRICE	NETT VALUE
4167	EGGSHELL WHITE GLOSS	300 Ltrs		4.00	1,200.00
4239	EGGSHELL BLACK GLOSS	300 Ltrs		4.00	1,200.00
4487	PINK VINYL SILK	50 Ltrs		4.20	210.00
					2,610.00

VAT RATE	GOODS AMOUNT	VAT AMOUNT
17.5%	2,610.00	456.75

Reg No.   884773
VAT Reg No. 8 991 487 5

2,610.00
456.75
3,066.75

1047

BLUEGRASS FARM

Chartwell
0293 661482

20 March 20X3

Woodright Ltd
324 Daisy Rd
Birmingham

	£
20 pints milk	6.00
1 sack potatoes	9.70
1 sack carrots	10.25
3 doz eggs	3.90
	29.85

RECEIVED

Inv No.	102844
Date	23/3/X3
Calcs (sign)	RS
Auth (sign)	PJM
NL Code	000 £29.85

Delivery To:

Woodright Ltd
324 Daisy Rd
Birmingham

BLIX

BLIX HARDWARE SUPPLIES
310-312 THE MARN
BIRMINGHAM
B19 OPS
061 887 400

INVOICE NO
R104793

Invoice To:

As above

Date	Carriage	Terms
18 April 20X3		30 DAYS NET

Description	Price	Amount
20,000 1" Nails	£10.00/1000	200.00
10,000 2" Nails	£12.00/1000	120.00
5,000 brackets	£0.25 each	1,250.00
		1,570.00
VAT @ 17.5%		274.75
		1,844.75

RECEIVED

Inv No.	103792
Date	20/4/X3
Calcs (sign)	
Auth (sign)	RS
NL Code	360 £1,250.00
	370 £320.00
	900 £274.75

Reg No 4671132   VAT No 3149827

Henhao Timber

INVOICE
47281170

Unit 6
Greycoat Estate
Ross-on-Wye
0429 91738

WOODRIGHT LTD
324 DAISY ROAD
BIRMINGHAM
B1 4LJ

DATE: 16.05.20X3
ACCOUNT: 107W004
TERMS: 7 DAYS NET

GOODS	QUANTITY	PRICE	AMOUNT
Grade 'A' Beechwood 6cm	4,000 m	£6.80/m	27,200.00
VAT	17.5%		4,760.00
			31,960.00

RECEIVED

Inv No.	104740
Date	17/5/X3
Calcs (sign)	RS
Auth (sign)	PJM
NL Code	180 £27,200.00
	900 £4,760.00

REG NO 1173458

VAT NO 84891173

17-19 May Road
Newcastle-upon-Tyne
NT23 1HQ

091 887 304

Ardwick
Accessories

INVOICE: 333147   **DATE:** 14.06.X3

Delivery date		WOODRIGHT LTD 324 DAISY ROAD BIRMINGHAM B1 4LJ	**Delivery Address (if different from invoice address)**
Account No **40156**			- - - - - - - - - -
Transport			

Code	Qty	Description	Amount
K1738	400	Brass door knobs	720.00
H3014	800	Brass hinges	400.00
KH317	400	Brass keyholes	260.00
LH118	400	Brass lock mechanisms	1,840.00
			3,220.00
		VAT at 17½ %	563.50
			3,783.50

RECEIVED

Inv No.	105688
Date	15/6/X3
Calcs (sign)	RS
Auth (sign)	PJM
NL Code	340 £3.220.00 900 £563.50

Reg No 117348   VAT No 1 0821179

To:			
WOODRIGHT LTD 324 DAISY ROAD BIRMINGHAM B1 4LJ	*Touch* *Of* *Glass*		33-38 Glass Road, Bursley Stoke on Trent 0923 147856

Date: 10 July 20X3		*Inv No:* 911734

	QTY	AMT
Security panels: reinforced glass	400	896.00
Glass cutters	400	532.00
		1,428.00
VAT (17.5%)		249.90
		1,677.90

RECEIVED

Inv No.	106636
Date	10/7/X3
Calcs (sign)	RS
Auth (sign)	PJM
NL Code	220 £896.00 240 £532.00 900 £249.90

Reg No 914 367	VAT No 1 472 1890

SALES INVOICE

MUSTAFA LTD

Acton Grange, Gloucestershire, GU11 4PS, 0693 71592

To:		
WOODRIGHT LTD 324 DAISY ROAD BIRMINGHAM B1 4LJ	*Date:* 11.08.X3 *Terms:* 7 DAYS NET	

DESCRIPTION	*QUANTITY*	*AMOUNT*
3 cm oak planks	40m	288.00
4 cm oak planks	30m	234.00
		522.00
VAT	17.5%	91.35
		613.35

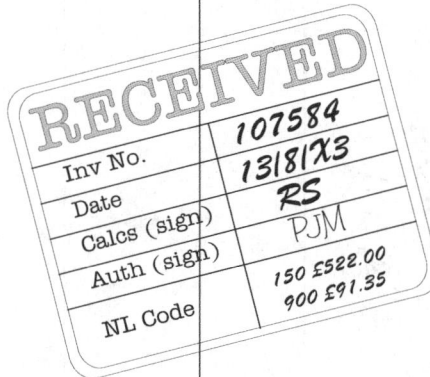

RECEIVED

Inv No.	107584
Date	13/8/X3
Calcs (sign)	RS
Auth (sign)	PJM
NL Code	150 £522.00 900 £91.35

REG NO   7499188   VAT NO   0119 469823

24

Paper March

Reg No : 31 74118
VAT No : 7 189 737 4

Recall House
Cardiff
Ct1 1AJ
Tel: 091 429 317

Date: 5 September 20X3

Invoice No: 4732

Our ref: W147
             WOODRIGHT LTD
             324 DAISY ROAD
             BIRMINGHAM
             B1 4LJ

To: 60 reams A4 Letterhead   360.00

        VAT at 17½%   63.00

        Amount due   423.00

RECEIVED

Inv No.	108532
Date	6/9/X3
Calcs (sign)	RS
Auth (sign)	PJM
NL Code	100 £360.00
	900 £63.00

Reg No. 124379
VAT Reg 9 114 867 5

**Shamrock
Supplies Ltd**

92 Cutters Yard, Liverpool,
Lancashire 0498 611732

WOODRIGHT LTD
324 DAISY RD
BIRMINGHAM
B1

INVOICE: 774/311849
DATE: 03.10.X3

GOODS	PRICE	VAT	QTY	AMT
2cm Chipboard 10m x 4m	£1.25	17.5	700 sqm	875.00
3cm MDF board 10m x 4m	£1.90	17.5	1,000 sqm	1,900.00

RECEIVED

Inv No.   109480
Date   8/10/X3
Calcs (sign) RS
Auth (sign) PJM
NL Code   620 £2,775.00
             900 £485.62

Sub Total				2,775.00
VAT				485.62
Total				3,260.62

SETTLEMENT DISCOUNT OF 2% FOR PAYMENT WITHIN 7 DAYS

WOODRIGHT LTD   19474

GOODS   RECEIVED   NOTE

SUPPLIER
Green Forest Timber

DATE: *29/1/X3*

RECEIVED BY: *RH*

GOODS : DESCRIPTION	QUANTITY
6cm Pine Planking	*500m*

WOODRIGHT LTD   19593

GOODS   RECEIVED   NOTE

SUPPLIER
Pots of Paint Ltd

DATE: *23/2/X3*

RECEIVED BY: *RH*

GOODS : DESCRIPTION	QUANTITY
Eggshell White	*300 Ltrs*
Eggshell Black	*300 Ltrs*
Vinyl Silk Pink	*50 Ltrs*

WOODRIGHT LTD

19738

GOODS   RECEIVED   NOTE

SUPPLIER

Bluegrass Farm
- Mrs Beavis

DATE: *20/3/X3*

RECEIVED BY: *RH*

GOODS : DESCRIPTION	QUANTITY
Eggs	*3 Doz*
Milk	*20 pints*
Potatoes	*1 Sack*
Carrots	*1 Sack*

WOODRIGHT LTD

19888

GOODS   RECEIVED   NOTE

SUPPLIER

Blix Hardware Supplies

DATE: *14/4/X3*

RECEIVED BY: *RH*

GOODS : DESCRIPTION	QUANTITY
1" Nails	*20,000*
2" Nails	*10,000*
Brackets	*5,000*

WOODRIGHT LTD

19975

GOODS   RECEIVED   NOTE

SUPPLIER
Henhao Timber

DATE: *15/5/X3*

RECEIVED BY: *RH*

GOODS : DESCRIPTION	QUANTITY
Grade 'A' 6cm Beechwood	*4,000m*

WOODRIGHT LTD

20059

GOODS   RECEIVED   NOTE

SUPPLIER
Ardwick Accessories

DATE: *12/6/X3*

RECEIVED BY: *RH*

GOODS : DESCRIPTION	QUANTITY
Brass Door Knobs	*400*
Brass Hinges	*800*
Brass Keyholes	*400*
Brass Lock Mechanisms	*400*

WOODRIGHT LTD

20310

GOODS   RECEIVED   NOTE

SUPPLIER

Touch of Glass

DATE: *6/7/X3*

RECEIVED BY: *RH*

GOODS : DESCRIPTION	QUANTITY
Glass Cutters	*400*

WOODRIGHT LTD

20196

GOODS   RECEIVED   NOTE

SUPPLIER

Touch of Glass

DATE: *9/7/X3*

RECEIVED BY: *RH*

GOODS : DESCRIPTION	QUANTITY
Security Panels	*400*

WOODRIGHT LTD

20430

GOODS   RECEIVED   NOTE

SUPPLIER

Mustafa Ltd

DATE: *9/8/X3*

RECEIVED BY: *RH*

GOODS : DESCRIPTION	QUANTITY
3cm Oak Planks	*30m*
4cm Oak Planks	*40m*

WOODRIGHT LTD

20556

GOODS   RECEIVED   NOTE

SUPPLIER

Paper March

DATE: *3/9/X3*

RECEIVED BY: *RH*

GOODS : DESCRIPTION	QUANTITY
Boxes of A4 letterhead *(1 Box = 3 Reams)*	*20*

WOODRIGHT LTD

20664

GOODS   RECEIVED   NOTE

SUPPLIER

Shamrock Supplies Ltd

DATE: *30/9/X3*

RECEIVED BY: *RH*

GOODS : DESCRIPTION	QUANTITY
2cm Chipboard 10m x 4m	*700 sq m*

WOODRIGHT LTD

20782

GOODS   RECEIVED   NOTE

SUPPLIER

Shamrock Supplies Ltd

DATE: *2/10/X3*

RECEIVED BY: *RH*

GOODS : DESCRIPTION	QUANTITY
3cm MDF board 10m x 4m	*1,000 sq m*

12 The computer systems in use by Zhong Ltd are set out in the notes of the accounting systems below. Zhong Ltd has two directors, Douglas and Allister. Identify the weaknesses apparent in the computerised accounting systems and set out these weaknesses in the form of a management letter to the directors of Zhong Ltd. Your letter should include introductory paragraphs but it does not need to include the normal concluding paragraphs.

Accounting Systems

Accounting systems are computerised apart from the stock records which are kept using a system of manual stock records. One of the developments planned for the next year will be to computerise the stock records and to upgrade and improve the computer systems which have tended to grow in a rather haphazard fashion over the years. For example, the wages records are kept on a separate stand alone PC which is not linked to the PC used for the other accounting functions.

The accounting functions use a version of Sage standard accounting software.

(a) **Sales**

Most sales are for cash. Customers send in orders using the order form supplied with the catalogue and either enclose payment or quote a credit card number. A considerable volume of credit card sales are taken over the telephone and in future Douglas would like to see the firm offering its products via the Internet. Allister strongly disagrees with this and also many other proposed administration developments, preferring that Zhong Ltd remains 'a traditional firm'.

Decisions to open credit accounts can only be taken by Douglas or Allister but no credit limits apply. As a result the firm has experienced some bad debts and delayed payments particularly from overseas customers allowed credit accounts. Any invoices are raised by the accounts clerk and sent with the goods. All customers for cash also receive a receipted invoice so that all sales are recorded as either cash sale invoices or credit sale invoices. Invoices are serially numbered when they are sent out.

(b) **Purchases**

The firm uses a network of high quality suppliers which it has built up over the years. Some suppliers have been pressing for quicker payments and Zhong has also suffered quality problems with one supplier in particular this year. This has lead to customer complaints and dissatisfaction, hence the move to manufacture 'in house' the items concerned.

Both directors raise orders and the storemen are also allowed to order items. No checks on incoming goods are considered necessary by the firm because 'we trust our suppliers'. The one exception to this is the supplier responsible for the faulty parts referred to above. When invoices arrive they are stapled to the purchase order, accumulated by supplier for monthly posting to the purchase ledger. The suppliers' accounts cheques are then raised by the accounts clerk and signed by either Douglas or Allister who are the only cheque signatories.

(c) **Wages**

All staff apart from the directors receive a weekly basic wage. All staff clock in and the accounts clerk prepares the weekly payroll using the stand-alone PC, payroll summary for input to the Sage accounting system and the wages cheque for signature. All the pay packets are assembled by the accounts clerk who draws the necessary cash from the bank, which is next-door, weekly.

An annual staff bonus is paid via the payroll and the amounts concerned are agreed by Douglas and Allister and notified to the accounts clerk.

(d) **Stock**

There are about 11,000 stock lines. The records are kept using a card index stock system. Each stock card records stock receipts, issues and the running balance. Each card bears a minimum stock and reorder level/quantity together with details of the supplier. Once the stock level reaches the reorder level an order is raised for the reorder quantity from the same supplier. No research is done into other possible suppliers and whether the order quantity is still appropriate.

There is an annual stock-take, which you attended.

Periodically also, the balances on the most popular stock lines should be reconciled to the actual stocks. However, this rarely happens because of the time it takes and also the generally disorganised state of the stores. The stock record cards also record the average cost of the stock items which is recalculated each time there is a new stock delivery.

(e) **Accounting matters**

There are control accounts for purchases and sales. There is also a weekly bank reconciliation by the accounts clerk who also agrees the shop cash floats. No payments are allowed to be made out of cash takings apart from any sums which Douglas and Allister might draw. Purchase and sales ledger balances are agreed to the control accounts each month. There are no monthly management accounts as such but the directors monitor sales and stock levels (to the best of their ability) on a monthly basis. They also scrutinise the bank statements when they are received.

The accounts have received a modified audit report in the past because of the stock problems referred to earlier.

Computer access is available to all staff. No password protection systems are in use.

All files are backed up regularly and back up copies are kept by the accounts clerk in her desk.

chapter 5:
ASSESSING RISKS

1   Why are auditors required to obtain an understanding of the entity and its environment?

2   What is audit risk and what are its three components?

3   What steps will an auditor take in assessing risks once he has gained an understanding of the entity and its environment?

4   What can go wrong at a financial statement level?

5   What is materiality, and how does it affect what an auditor does?

6   What makes a risk significant?

7   How much evidence does an auditor need to obtain?

8   What procedures will auditors use to carry out tests of detail and what specifically are they obtaining evidence about?

9   Using the background information given below and your knowledge of the systems of Glad Rags Limited, identify two areas of risk for the audit and explain why they are risks.

Background information

Glad Rags Limited is a private company set up by Bill and Gladys Burton 50 years ago. It manufactures clothes which it sells mainly to High Street Clothing Stores. The company relies heavily on two major customers: British Clothes Stores and Value Mart. The company has another 20 customers on the sales ledger, but BCS and VM account for 60% of turnover. BCS have recently told Gladys that they are auditing their suppliers to ensure that the suppliers meet their stringent quality requirements. Glad Rags has three major suppliers (Fine Fabrics, The Fabric Wholesaler and Terry's Threads).

The company is 100% owned by Gladys Burton, who inherited her husband's shares when he died in 20X0. She is the sole director. Gladys has no children to inherit the business and has confided to the auditors that she is thinking of selling the business in the near future. Her plans are not known to any other members of staff at Glad Rags.

Your audit firm has been the auditor for 5 years. The firm has always found Gladys to be honest and reliable. Gladys has a key role in the day to day running of the business. She oversees the production of the company sales catalogue, runs the personnel department (hiring and firing staff and dealing with the payroll) and determines which suppliers the company will use.

Turnover is £7 million with gross profit at 30% and net profit of 9.5%.

Gladys employs a part-time bookkeeper (Bill Overton) to oversee the two accounts assistants (Jane and Beth) and to produce monthly and annual accounts. Including these staff members and Gladys, there are 8 administrative staff and 50 machinists/cutters.

Materiality has been set at £70,000 for this year's audit.

10   Link the risks you have identified above to what could go wrong at a financial statement level.

11   Using the balance sheet below, identify what items will require audit testing, giving explanations.

BALANCE SHEET FOR GLAD RAGS LIMITED
Year ended 30 November 20X4

	20X4 £	20X4 £	20X3 £	20X3 £
Fixed assets		21,940		24,794
Current assets				
Stock	352,599		302,214	
Debtors	1,345,933		1,412,911	
Bank	29,583	1,757,698	23,491	1,738,616
Net current assets		1,779,638		1,763,410
Creditors: amounts falling due				
within one year		(365,038)		(355,893)
		1,414,600		1,407,517
Capital and reserves				
Share capital		1,000		1,000
Profit and loss account		1,413,600		1,408,517
		1,414,600		1,407,517

12   Using the accounting systems information about sales at Greenfingers Limited given in the questions to Chapter 3, identify a factor which increases the likelihood of error in the financial statements, explaining why this may lead to an error or misstatement.

13 The accountant at Greenfingers has presented you with a draft balance sheet for the year, which is given below. The audit manager has suggested that it is likely that materiality will be set at £65,000. Identify which balances below should be tested in detail and which should be reviewed.

Draft balance sheet for Greenfingers Limited year ended 31 December 20X4				
		20X4		20X3
	£	£	£	£
Fixed assets		3,812,594		3,862,591
Current assets				
Stock	423,781		405,863	
Debtors	10,020		9,930	
Bank balance	–		25,795	
		433,801		441,588
Current liabilities				
Bank overdraft	(17,000)			
Trade creditors	(226,313)		(220,879)	
Accruals	(32,476)		(29,583)	
Bank loan	(100,000)		(100,000)	
		(365,789)		(350,462)
Long term liabilities				
Bank loan		(2,425,000)		(2,525,000)
		1,455,606		1,428,717

14 You are the audit senior on Excellentia plc, a large manufacturing company, and are currently planning the audit. Your senior assistant on the assignment is helping you plan the work as he has never been involved in planning an audit before. Excellentia plc has an internal audit department.

The company has provided you with some draft figures to assist you with the planning of the audit.

Task 1

Explain to your assistant the main administrative matters that the audit strategy should cover. Your answer should include consideration of the timing of significant parts of the audit process.

Task 2

Explain, using the draft information that the client has given you, why the following areas of the accounts will require investigation during the final audit.

(a) Liquidity
(b) Tangible fixed assets and activity
(c) Sales and debtors
(d) Stocks and activity

	£'000	£'000
Tangible fixed assets (at net book value)	22,350	22,175
Stocks: raw materials	1,100	1,000
work in progress	400	500
finished goods	5,500	4,000
Debtors	4,800	5,200
Creditors	(2,800)	(3,000)
Bank overdraft	(1,900)	(1,400)
Turnover	28,000	25,500
Cost of sales *	(20,000)	(18,700)
	8,000	6,800
Distribution cost *	(3,300)	(3,200)
Administrative expenses *	(2,200)	(2,100)
Profit before taxation	2,500	1,500
* Depreciation included in these figures	2,000	1,800

Task 3

As there are considerable pressures on audit fees this year, the audit partner would like you to recommend improvements in audit efficiency. He believes that one possible improvement may be to use computer-assisted audit techniques. However he does not know much about these, and has asked you how the main techniques might be used.

Summarise for the audit partner the main purposes and features of test data and audit software.

15   Complete the table below. In the left-hand column you should list the financial statement assertions and in the right-hand column give an example of a test that fulfils each assertion.

Financial statement assertion	Example test

16   During your pre-planning visit to Asoka Ltd, the finance director gives you a draft profit and loss account (income statement) to assist you in your planning work. This is set out below. The figures are based on internal management information for the first eleven months of the year, and budgeted figures for the last month of the year. You know from reading previous years' audit files

that draft accounts prepared at a similar time on a similar basis have generally proved to be a reliable indication of the final figures for the year.

Task

Perform analytical procedures on the profit and loss account figures, comparing 20X8 to 20X7 on a percentage basis, gross and net profit percentages between 20X8 and 20X7, and each category of expenses (e.g. finance charges) as a % of sales. Highlight significant variations which will require further investigation during the audit and indicate what procedures should be carried out in respect of them. Significant variations include all variations greater than 10% where the 20X8 expense is greater than £20,000. You should use the draft accounts set out on pages to give details of % changes and items requiring further investigation. You should also prepare a working paper, giving the test objective, the work done, the results and the conclusions drawn.

DRAFT PROFIT AND LOSS ACCOUNT			
	20X8	*% change*	*20X7*
	£		£
Turnover	11,536,088		14,315,053
Cost of sales (including manufacturing costs)	10,271,247		12,260,507
Gross profit	1,264,841		2,054,546
Gross profit %			
	20X8	*% change*	*20X7*
Administration and establishment charges	£		£
Directors' remuneration	272,650		206,567
Computer charges	35,410		34,524
Incidental expenses	23,796		26,533
Insurance	68,992		49,889
Legal and other professional fees	40,327		18,000
Printing, postage and stationery	24,553		23,817
Repairs and renewals	42,168		41,125
Telephone	28,980		27,153
Depreciation	2,051		5,268
Loss/(profit) on foreign exchange	20,227		(59,122)
(Profit) on sale of fixed assets	(30,080)		–
	529,074		373,754
Less: Rent received	70,000		70,000
	459,074		303,754
% of turnover			

	20X8	% change	20X7
Finance charges	£		£
Audit	26,250		13,125
Accountancy	8,750		5,250
Bank charges	6,024		5,562
Loan interest	33,250		33,250
Bad debts	92,568		13,832
	166,842		71,019
Less: Interest received	36,155		45,486
	130,687		25,533

% of turnover

	20X8	% change	20X7
Manufacturing costs (in cost of sales)	£		£
Wages	1,938,937		2,180,780
Social Security Costs	193,970		218,120
Machine and maintenance	37,853		48,311
Light, heat and power	103,995		114,593
Rent	192,500		140,000
Business rates	11,186		10,444
Hire of machinery	9,958		18,942
Depreciation	79,683		42,455
Machinery expenses	25,287		–
	2,593,369		2,773,645

% of turnover

	20X8	% change	20X7
Selling and distribution charges	£		£
Travelling and entertaining expenses	35,434		27,465
Motor expenses	35,277		25,326
Depreciation	62,664		51,089
Advertising and trade fairs	51,544		40,758
Commission	5,446		6,751
	190,365		151,389

% of turnover

chapter 6:
AUDIT PLANNING

1 What is the difference between the audit strategy and the audit plan?

2 You are an audit senior working with a new trainee, Jenny.

Task 1

For Jenny's benefit, explain how, and in consultation with whom, the audit strategy is formulated.

Task 2

You and Jenny will be doing some on-site audit work next week. Explain the concepts of 'direction', 'supervision' and 'review' in the context of the audit team.

3 What will the audit team discuss at a planning meeting?

4 An audit strategy states that the auditors need to use the work of an expert to obtain evidence about a particular aspect of the financial statements. What matters will the auditors consider before using the work of that expert?

5 What practical matters must the auditors deal with if they want to make use of the work of the company's internal audit department?

6 Company X wishes to establish an internal audit function but there is probably only 2½ days a week of work involved.

The company has identified Rozina, who works in the market research department. She has A levels in accountancy and business studies. The marketing department is currently overstaffed and the directors have suggested that perhaps Rozina might be able to 'wear two hats' by splitting her work load between market research and internal audit. It is proposed that Rozina spends the morning in market research then in the afternoon she moves to a new office set up for her from which she will run the internal audit function.

Task

As the external auditor, explain what criteria you would take into consideration in assessing the status of the proposed internal audit function and whether you could make use of the internal audit work performed by Rozina.

7 When might auditors use the work of another auditor?

8   You are currently auditing the group financial statements of Big Ted plc. Big Ted has one major subsidiary, Little Tortoise Ltd, which is audited by another firm of auditors.

Task

Describe the procedures that you will need to carry out in order to be able to rely on the work of the auditors of Little Tortoise Ltd.

9   What factors must an auditor consider when selecting a sample?

10 You are an audit senior on the audit of Gemma Ltd. Materiality has been set at £20,000. The manager has set a sample size of 10 for the debtors circularisation.

Task

Select a sample from the sales ledger listing given below, giving reasons for your selection.

SALES LEDGER LISTING	£
Affectionado Ltd	76,002
Astra Stones Ltd	491
B. Trow Ltd	34,726
Bea Myan Ltd	7,013
Crystal Eyes plc	12,997
Engagement Centre Ltd	16,821
Gemba-Gems Ltd	22,032
Gemeyma Ltd	17,152
Jewels 'r' us Ltd	3,294
Love Me Tender Ltd	6,111
Manifique Ltd	987
Moonglow Ltd	1,342
Pearly Kween Ltd	812
Ruby-Dubie Ltd	467
Ring-ring Ltd	12,142
Wed-Me Ltd	8,429
	220,818

11 You are the audit senior for the audit of Glad Rags. You will be assisted by Jules Devoran, who is relatively new to the firm and has little audit experience.

The audit manager has asked you to compile a memo to Jules, explaining the typical contents of an audit strategy, and in particular, the matters that he should expect to see covered in the Glad Rags audit strategy.

12   The manager has determined that a debtors' circularisation will be carried out as part of the audit of Glad Rags Limited. Jules will be attending the client at the year end to organise the debtors' circularisation. However, the manager has asked you to select a sample for the circularisation. Materiality is £70,000 and the sample size has been set at 8. The list of balances at the year end is given below. You should include a memo with the sample telling Jules why you have picked that sample.

	£
Allways Stores Limited	31,486
Baby Stores Limited	29,472
British Clothes Stores plc	484,536
Brodies	74,973
Cavanaghs Limited	14,388
Desert Fashions Limited	32,593
High Street Fashion Limited	22,711
House of Blazer plc	29,077
H and T Limited	18,933
More Clothes Limited	11,852
Natasha Phillips Limited	41,894
Naturals Limited	11,852
Nice Clothes Limited	17,231
Pristine Fashions plc	6,893
Really Nice Dress Company Limited	34,893
The Fashion Store plc	31,946
Tisco Stores plc	78,805
Value Clothes Limited	22,315
Value Mart	323,024
Wearable Classics Ltd	13,042
	1,345,933

13   Now you have completed the pre-planning work at Greenfingers Limited, you will be drafting the audit strategy for approval by the audit partner. Set out the matters that will be included within that strategy document.

1   What company control is a key factor in determining whether the stocks in the financial statements actually exist?

2   What problems can arise if the stock cut-off is incorrect?

3   When auditing the value of finished goods, what components of cost will auditors need to verify, and how are they likely to be able to test those components?

4   What tests should the auditors carry out to ensure that net realisable value of stock is higher than cost?

5   When Jules attends Glad Rags Limited at the yearend, he is going to attend the annual stocktake. The audit manager has asked you to plan the stocktake attendance for Jules. Using the information given below, appraise the key issues for Jules at the stocktake and identify any stock which he should include within his test counts.

You should also appraise the stocktake instructions provided by the company to ascertain whether you believe the stocktake is capable of producing a reliable figure for the existence of stock.

Last year's working papers show that the major items in stock were standard white thread (code: S01) and cotton jersey fabric in black and blue (codes: CJ02 and CJ03). The sample size for test counts was 12.

MEMO

From: Joe Worple, Stores Manager, Glad Rags Limited
To: Audit senior

I enclose the instructions for this year's stock count, which will take place at 3pm on 30 November. The machines will not be operating during the count. Ten machinists have volunteered to be counters, the rest have accepted a half-day.

There are no new issues relating to stock this year, except that the company has just bought a large consignment of specialist fabric A001 to service a large order for Value Mart. The reorder levels for most of the standard fabrics have not changed from last year. In December, we shall be starting some major orders for clients for the spring season, so we have a high level of stock as usual. As you know, our fabric and threads are measured in metres and the bales are marked up with lengths removed. We do not remeasure every bale of fabric.

Most of the fabric and threads are in the stores. The machinists will be asked to finish work in progress at the end of the day before the stocktake. There will be some goods awaiting delivery which are kept in the machining room. We are not planning to make any deliveries on the day of the stocktake and have requested that our suppliers do not make deliveries on the day.

GLAD RAGS LIMITED

STOCK COUNT INSTRUCTIONS 30 November 20X4

Overseer – Joe Worple, Stores Manager

Checkers – Betty Fradin, Liz Tyler, Mandeep Singh, Bet King, Elspeth Worthing, Jill Manson, Jane Smith, Bev Jones, Claire King, Ann Jones

All pieces should be finished before the stocktake commences. Machinists should not commence new pieces after 2pm. All finished goods need to be placed in the east end of the machine room to be counted.

Checkers should work in pairs and will be allocated to different areas of the stores. Two checkers will count finished goods in the machine room. Each checker will be issued with a sheet stating the fabrics and threads in their section which they must count. One checker should check the amounts of each fabric and write them down on the sheet. Once a bale has been counted, it must be marked with a red sticker to show that it has been counted. The second checker should check the first checker's work. When an item has been checked for a second time, it should be marked with a green sticker. Joe Worple will carry out random checks on completed stocksheets to ensure that items have been checked correctly.

Each checking pair should remeasure four bales of fabric to ensure that the record attached to the bale is correct.

No checker must leave until permitted by Joe Worple. Checkers will be paid £6 an hour for the count, which must be noted and authorised by Joe Worple.

6   It is now the final audit of Glad Rags Limited. The stock cut-off information which Jules obtained at the stocktake is given below. Jules has obtained follow up information to establish whether cut off is correct, but is unsure what conclusion he should draw. Draw a conclusion whether the stock cut off is correct, stating any further work required, if applicable.

Client:	Glad Rags Ltd	Prepared by:	J Devoran
Accounting date:	30 November 20X4	Date:	2 January 20X5
		Reviewed by:	
		Date:	

Stock cut off

Last deliveries out

Sales order/GDN	Customer	Agreed to November Sales Day Book
200894/DN12403	Value Mart	✓
200895/DN12404	BCS	✓
200896/DN12405	Tisco Stores	✓

The above items have all been excluded from the stock count

Last deliveries in (from invoices pending file – these were the only three orders received pending invoices)

Order	Supplier	Agreed to November Purchase Day Book
P1013	Fine Fabrics Ltd	✓
P1017	Fine Fabrics Ltd	✓
P1021	Terry's Threads	*

* This invoice was not received until 15 December and was included in December's Purchase Day Book. The value was £2,476.

All the above items were included in the stock count.

7   Below are the results of the testing that Jules did at the stock take of Glad Rags Limited. Write a note to Jules stating what further work needs to be carried out at the final audit to ensure that the existence of stock is fairly stated.

Client:	Glad Rags Ltd		Prepared by:	J Devoran
Accounting date:	30 November 20X4		Date:	30 November 20X4
			Reviewed by:	
			Date:	

Stock existence

Items remeasured

Stock code	Amount per record	Amount measured	Correct
C01	20.75m	20.75m	Yes
L02	13.45m	13.45m	Yes
S03	2.5m	2.5m	Yes
CJ04	16.75m	16.75m	Yes
CJ05	2.35m	2.35m	Yes

Arithmetical accuracy of records

Stock code	Record adds?
L01	Yes
L03	Yes
S05	Yes

Conclusion – controls over stock measurement operate effectively

Test counts

Stock code	Amount per stock sheet	Amount physically present	Count correct?
A001	200m	200m	Yes
S01	4 × 50m	4 × 50m	Yes
	1 × 21m	1 × 21m	
CJ02	2 × 50m	2 × 50m	Yes
	1 × 1.35m	1 × 1.35m	
CJ03	2 × 50m	2 × 50m	Yes
	1 × 25.50m	1 × 25.50m	
CJ04	16.75m	16.75m	Yes
S02	4 × 50m	4 × 50m	Yes
	1 × .25m	1 × .25m	
L04	12m	12m	Yes
N01	135m	135m	Yes
N02	127m	127m	Yes
X101 White t-shirts	250	250	Yes
X103 Blue t-shirts	175	175	Yes
Z111 Babygros	1,000	1,000	Yes

Conclusion – test counts indicate count operated efficiently

8 Jules has now completed the work on existence of stock at Glad Rags and has found that stock existence is fairly stated. You will be carrying out the work on the valuation of stock. The sample you have selected is shown below. Using the purchase invoices and catalogue extracts also given below, you should carry out the audit of stock valuation. On your working paper, you should set out the objectives of your test, the work you have done and draw a conclusion.

Sample for stock valuation test

Stock code	Description	Quantity	Total value
A001	Special	200m	1,200
CJ03	Cotton jersey – blue	221m	265
N01	Nylon – white	135m	169
Z111	Babygros	1,000	5,350
X102	T-shirts – red	2,000	6,200
X204	BMC Skirts – red	12,000	120,000

Purchase invoices

FINE FABRICS LIMITED

Unit 12 Marlowe Industrial Park Marlowe	To: Glad Rags Limited The Old Mill Forseby	VAT registration: 012 2345 56

Invoice: 33155
Date: 11 Nov 20X4

Item	Quantity	Unit price	Price
Cotton jersey blue	1000m	1.20	1,200.00
Nylon white	1000m	1.25	1,250.00
VAT @ 17.5%			428.75
TOTAL			2,878.75

THE FABRIC WHOLESALER

Invoice to:	Glad Rags Limited, The Old Mill, Foresby
Invoice date:	26 November 20X4
Invoice number:	SI1103

Item		Unit price	Net	VAT	Total
A001	200m	6.00	1,200	210	1,410

4, The Ridge, Overhill, OV12 8RL

VAT Registration number: 933 9345 925

Catalogue extracts

Item	Description	Unit cost
X10 (1/2/3/4)	Ladies plain t-shirts, available in white (1), black (2), blue (3), and red (4). Sizes S/M/L	4.00
X10L(1/2/3/4)	Ladies plain t-shirts, available in white (1), black (2), blue (3), and red (4). Sizes XL/XXL	5.00
X11(1/2/3/4)	Men's plain t-shirts, available in white (1), black (2), blue (3), and red (4). Sizes S/M/L	5.00
X11L(1/2/3/4)	Men's plain t-shirts, available in white (1), black (2), bluc (3), and rcd (4). Sizcs XL/XXL	6.00
Z111	Babygro white. Sizes NB/3/6/9/12	12.00
Z113	Babygro blue. Sizes NB/3/6/9/12	12.00
Z115	Babygro pink. Sizes NB/3/6/9/12	12.00
X20(1/2/3/4)	Ladies BCS skirts, available in white (1) black (2), blue (3) and red (4). Sizes S/M/L	15.00

9   You are planning the audit of Caterpillar Computers Ltd. The audit manager has asked you to draft the stock section of the audit strategy.

Task 1

Describe the work that should be carried out before the start of the stocktake.

Task 2

State the principal procedures that should be covered in the company's stocktaking instructions.

Task 3

Describe the procedures that should be carried out and the items that should be recorded at the stocktake.

Task 4

Describe the procedures that should be carried out at the final audit to check that the company has implemented proper cut-off for stock.

Task 5

State the main categories of stock for which the net realisable value is likely to be less than cost, and describe how to identify stock that may be worth less than cost (Note: you are not required to describe how the net realisable value of this stock should be determined).

chapter 8:
AUDIT OF OTHER ASSETS
(AND RELATED ITEMS)

1 What audit tests should be carried out over completeness of fixed assets?

2 What factors will an auditor consider when auditing valuation of fixed assets?

3 It is 10 November 20X3 and you have been asked to work on the audit of the fixed asset section of the accounts of Kandistors Limited for the year ended 31 December 20X3. The company manufactures sweets and chocolate which it sells and delivers to the retail trade.

The partner in charge of the audit has asked you to examine the fixed assets section of the company's most recent management accounts. The company maintains a fixed assets register and you should assume that there will be no fixed asset acquisitions between the dates of 1 November 20X3 and 31 December 20X3.

Task

Prepare a fixed assets audit plan of work, detailing TEN audit procedures to be carried out to meet the following assertions:

Completeness
Existence
Valuation
Ownership
Presentation and disclosure

You are not required to consider disposals of fixed assets or depreciation charges.

For each procedure mentioned in your programme where appropriate you should identify the associated assertion.

4 What balances must an auditor not neglect when selecting a sample for auditing debtors?

5 Why do auditors often use analytical procedures to test sales?

6 When should auditors send out the bank letter request?

7 What is window dressing?

8 You are continuing your work at Glad Rags Limited.

The debtors circularised at the yearend are listed below. Using the information given below, complete the work on debtors. Your working paper should set out the objectives of the test, the work done, the results and the conclusion.

Sample

British Clothes Stores plc	484,536
Brodies	74,973
Tisco Stores plc	78,805
Value Mart	323,024
Cavanaghs Limited	14,388
H and T Limited	18,933
Nice Clothes Limited	17,231
Value Clothes Limited	22,315

Debtors circularisation replies

Auditors
High Street
Townville

Dear Sirs

Amount owed to GLAD RAGS LIMITED

Except as noted below, we confirm we owe a balance of :   £74,973
At: 30 November 20X4

Name of business: Brodies Limited
Signed: Jane Withers   Position: Purchase ledger clerk
Date: 13 December 20X4

Exceptions:

Auditors
High Street
Townville

Dear Sirs

Amount owed to GLAD RAGS LIMITED

Except as noted below, we confirm we owe a balance of :   £78,805
At: 30 November 20X4

Name of business: Tisco Stores plc
Signed: *Peter Waters*   Position: *Accountant*
Date: *16 December 20X4*

Exceptions: *Credit requested re invoice SI-12950 goods damaged.*
                     We owe a balance of £77,698

Auditors
High Street
Townville

Dear Sirs

Amount owed to GLAD RAGS LIMITED

Except as noted below, we confirm we owe a balance of :   £323,034
At: 30 November 20X4

Name of business: Tisco Stores plc
Signed: Jack Walters   Position: Accountant
Date: 23 December 20X4

Exceptions:

Auditors
High Street
Townville

Dear Sirs

Amount owed to GLAD RAGS LIMITED

Except as noted below, we confirm we owe a balance of :   £14,388
At: 30 November 20X4

Name of business: Cavanaghs Ltd
Signed: J Darby   Position: Accounts assistant
Date: 22 December 20X4

Exceptions:

Auditors
High Street
Townville

Dear Sirs

Amount owed to GLAD RAGS LIMITED

Except as noted below, we confirm we owe a balance of :   £22,315
At: 30 November 20X4

Name of business: Value Clothes
Signed: J Roberts   Position::   Purchase ledger clerk
Date: 3 December 20x4

Exceptions:

Cashbook (receipts) extracts

Date	Details	Amount £
1 Dec 20X4	BCS sales ledger	44,938
10 Dec 20X4	H and T sales ledger	8,934
14 Dec 20X4	Nice Clothes sales ledger	7,392
12 Jan 20X4	H and T sales ledger	9,999
18 Jan 20X4	Nice Clothes sales ledger	9,839

9 You have asked Jules if he will carry out the audit work on valuation of debts of Glad Rags. Jane Hill will be able to provide him with an aged debt analysis from the sales ledger at 30 November 20X4.

Jules has never audited valuation of debts before and is unsure what tests he should carry out. Write a note to Jules, setting out the work he should perform on debt valuation.

10 Below is a schedule of fixed assets at Greenfingers Limited. Set out the tests that should be done to verify that the fixed assets figure in the financial statements is true and fair. You have already verified the opening figures to the prior year audit file.

	Land £	Buildings £	Vehicles £	Fittings £	Total £
Cost at					
1 January 20X4	1,500,000	2,750,000	128,970	121,173	4,500,143
Additions	–	–	42,000	697	42,697
Cost at					
31 December 20X4	1,500,000	2,750,000	170,970	121,870	4,542,840
Accumulated depreciation					
at 1 January 20X4	–	503,000	66,893	67,659	637,552
Depreciation	–	55,000	25,646	12,048	92,694
Accumulated depreciation					
at 31 December 20X4	–	558,000	92,539	79,707	730,246
Net book value at					
1 January 20X4	1,500,000	2,247,000	62,077	53,514	3,862,591
Net book value at					
31 December 20X4	1,500,000	2,192,000	78,431	42,163	3,812,594

Depreciation rates:

Buildings – 2%
Vehicles – 15%
Fittings – 10%

11 You have the following information about Greenfingers' sales from the prior year audit file:

Sales income	Shop 1	Shop 2	Shop 3	Café
High season	Average 400 customers per day @ £30			
Mid seasons	Average 300 customers per day @ £20	Average 75% of income of shop 1	Average 65% of income of shop 1	Average ½ customers of shop 1 per day @ £8
Low season	Average 200 customers per day @ £15			

Sales mix		
Plants	65% of shop sales	Gross margin 35%
Hardware	35% of shop sales	Gross margin 25%
Café		Gross margin 60%
Overall gross profit margin from shops		31.5%

Using the sales and profit analysis the accountant at Greenfingers has provided you with for the year ending 31 December 20X4 (given below), perform analytical procedures on the sales total of £6,656,013 and the overall gross profit of £2,222,049, drawing a conclusion as to the truth and fairness of the sales and gross profit figures.

Sales and profit analysis for the year ending 31 December 20X4

	Shop 1	Shop 2	Shop 3	Cafe
Month	£	£	£	
January	91,814	68,721	59,665	24,526
February	187,699	140,962	122,004	36,612
March	183,352	141,181	119,729	36,626
April	367,354	271,842	236,943	48,574
May	372,732	279,176	244,773	49,004
June	369,572	277,623	240,998	48,764
July	367,324	275,493	242,801	49,221
August	185,388	142,193	116,609	36,455
September	185,341	139,376	119,545	36,589
October	92,864	68,354	59,495	24,467
November	93,519	68,684	59,990	24,776
December	93,041	68,895	60,948	24,399
Gross profit	815,850	611,888	530,303	264,008

12 Using the information given below and on the following page, audit the bank reconciliation for Greenfingers Limited at 31 December 20X4. Clare has verified the relevant figures to the cashbook and the bank letter.

```
BANK RECONCILIATION
31 December 20X4
                                                              £
Balance per cashbook                        CB          (17,000)
Less: 31 Dec takings                                     (1,278)
Add: Cheque payments      003465                          5,398
                          003466                          2,476
                          003467                         15,398
                          003468                            108
                          003469                          2,365
                          003470                          3,465
                          003471                            791
                          003472                             23
Balance per bank statement                  B           11,746

Key:
B – agreed to bank letter
CB – agreed to cashbook
```

THE NATIONAL BANK

24 High Street
Greenfingers Limited
Statement number 285
The Old Stables
Greenville

Business account: 02085774

Date		Payments £	Receipts £	Total £
Balance brought forward 1.1.20X5				11,746.01
4.1.X5	Credit receipts		884	
4.1.X5	Cash deposit 01547		394	13,024.01
5.1.X5	003468	108		
	003471	791		
	003472	23		12,102.01
	Credit receipts		683	
	Cash deposit 01548		665	13,450.01
6.1.X5	003465	5,398		
	003466	2,476		
	003467	15,398		(9,822.01)
	Credit receipts		345	
	Cash deposit 01549		940	(8,537.01)
7.1.X5	003470	3,465		(12002.01)
	Credit receipts		893	
	Cash deposit 01550		433	(10,676.01)
10.1.X5	003468	2,365		(13,041.01)
	Credit receipts		576	
	Cash deposit 01551		722	(11,743.01)

13 You are the audit assistant on the audit of Tiffenies, a company that delivers lunch to offices in the city centre. Tiffenies has a number of corporate clients to whom they extend significant credit. You have been assigned the audit of debtors, which is material to the balance sheet. At the year end you visited Tiffenies to conduct a debtors' circularisation, and have compiled the results to date in a working paper.

The audit supervisor, Lucy Leung, is visiting the site tomorrow and you need to finish the audit of this section and put together a memorandum of points arising together before she arrives. The credit controller is of the opinion that it is not worth re-circularising clients as historically there has been a very poor response rate to circularisation. You have reviewed previous years' files and confirmed that this the case.

Various of your working papers relating to the debtors audit are given on the next few pages. The total value of debtors in the balance sheet is £60,124.

Task 1

Complete a working paper drawing conclusions about the results of the debtors' circularisation and the further work that should be undertaken to complete this work on trade debtors.

Task 2

Using information given to you below, carry out the further work you advised in Task 1.

Task 3

Draft any management letter points which you consider are relevant in relation to the debtors audit.

Task 4

Complete a memorandum to Lucy Leung summarising the work that has been done on debtors, the problems arising, any further work which should be completed and any implications you feel exist for the audit report.

Working papers relating to debtors   **H30**

Client: **Tiffenies**

A/c date: 31 March 20X2
Prepared by: ME   Date: 30 May 20X2
Reviewed by: Date:

Sales system notes

It was observed during the course of the audit testing that customers are regularly allowed to exceed their credit limits. Debts are often outstanding for more than 90 days, although the invoiced terms are 60 days. Sales statements are not sent out to customers. Sangita, who acts as credit controller as well as invoicing clerk, only chases a debt if it is more than 120 days old.

Client:	Tiffenies
A/c date:	31 March 20X2
Prepared by:	ME
Reviewed by:	

Date:
Date:

H20

Debtors' circularisation

31 May 20X2

A/c code	Name	Balance £	Credit limit £	Confirmed?	Balance confirmed (if different) £	Reconciled? £	After date cash received?	Fairly stated?
AND01	Andropov	1,567	1,000					
BAK02	Baker and Co	3,487	3,000					
FAZ01	Faiza Associates	2,611	2,500		2,510	H21		
FRE04	Freshleys Ltd	6,499	6,000	✓				
GAX01	Gao and Co	984	750	✓				
PEA01	Peacock and Lorenzo	3,124	3,000					
PIT01	Pitmans	4,598	4,500	✓				
TAB02	Table Partnership	1,204	1,000		985	H21		
TRA01	Transnational Ltd	12,045	12,000					
AIM01	Zaidi	3,994	3,750					
		40,113						

Client: **Tiffenies**

A/c date: 31 March 20X2
Prepared by: ME   Date: 5.6.X2
Reviewed by: Date:

Reconciliation of debtors circularisation replies

Faiza Associates

	£
Balance per sales ledger:	2,611
Balance per reply:	2,510
Difference:	101

Difference represented by credit note issued on 29 March 20X2 for lunch which had gone off. Verified to credit note.

Table Partnership

	£
Balance per sales ledger:	1,204
Balance per reply:	985
Difference:	219

Part of the difference is represented by a credit note for £45 issued on 28 March for lunch which had gone off. Verified to credit note. Unable to reconcile the remaining difference of £174.

Extracts from Tiffenies' cash receipts book, April/May/June 20X2

Date	Customer	A/c Number	Cash receipt
2 Apr	TP	TAB02	£174
	Baker	BAK02	£1,238
	Wrigges	WRI01	£24
	Kadsins	KAD01	£302
	Smithsons	SMI05	£29
3 Apr	Peacock	PEA01	£3,124
8 Apr	Gao	GAT01	£100
12 Apr	Zaidi	AIM01	£1,477
22 Apr	Jones & Co	JON01	£4,566
25 Apr	Putmanns	PUT01	£29
30 Apr	Rowlands	ROW01	£1,298
2 May	Wrigges	WRI01	£69
	Kadsins	KAD01	£142
	Smithsons	SMI05	£33
3 May	Peacock	PEA01	£2,999
7 May	Baker	BAK02	£1,157
10 May	Zaidi	AIM01	£1,396
13 May	Pedleys	PED01	£1200
31 May	Andropov	AND01	£630

Sales ledger account breakdowns

Account no:	AND01		
Account name:	Andropov		
Date	*Invoice no*	£	£
B/f		167	
12.12.X1	1202166	254	
14.01.X2	0102134	376	
13.02.X2	0202135	442	
28.02.X2	CHQ20138		167
12.03.X2	0302149	495	
15.04.X2	0402166	398	
13.05.X2	0502141	441	
31.05.X2	CHQ50048		630

Account no:	BAK02		
Account name:	Baker and Co		

Date	Invoice no	£	£
B/f		2,063	
02.12.X1	1201003	313	
09.12.X1	1201124	287	
15.12.X1	1201189	299	
23.12.X1	1201255	323	
04.01.X2	CHQ12011		987
07.01.X2	0102021	255	
14.01.X2	0102133	359	
21.01.X2	0102198	333	
28.01.X2	0102244	291	
01.02.X2	CHQ01334		1,022
04.02.X2	0202015	298	
11.02.X2	0202111	302	
18.02.X2	0202154	213	
25.02.X2	0202200	344	
01.03.X2	CHQ3001		1,254
04.03.X2	0302023	323	
11.03.X2	0302098	277	
18.03.X2	0302166	300	
25.03.X2	0302212	170	
01.04.X2	0402001	322	
01.04.X2	CHQ40002		1,238
08.04.X2	0402099	267	
15.04.X2	0402175	319	
22.04.X2	0402233	298	
29.04.X2	0402287	353	
06.05.X2	CHQ50011		1,157
06.05.X2	0502021	312	
13.05.X2	0502142	286	
20.05.X2	0502166	307	
27.05.X2	0502222	341	

Account no:	PEA01		
Account name:	Peacock and Lorenzo		

Date	Invoice no	£	£
B/f		3,456	
03.12.X2	CHQ12013		3,456
12.12.X1	1201168	1,567	
31.12.X1	1201276	1,494	
08.01.X2	CHQ10045		3,061
16.01.X2	0102151	1,399	
30.01.X2	0102258	1,596	
06.02.X2	CHQ20023		2,995
13.02.X2	0202133	1,678	
27.02.X2	0202234	1,386	
05.03.X2	CHQ30002		3,064
06.03.X2	0302043	1,594	
20.03.X2	0302184	1,530	
03.04.X2	CHQ40008		3,124
03.04.X2	0402023	1,601	
17.04.X2	0402207	1,398	
03.05.X2	CHQ50001		2,999
17.05.X2	0502179	1,345	
31.05.X2	0502227	1,529	

Account no:	TRA01		
Account name:	Transnational Ltd		

Date	Invoice no	£	£
23.12.X1	1201256	11,150	
23.12.X1	1201257	895	

| Account no: | AIM01 | | |
| Account name: | Zaidi | | |

Date	Invoice no	£	£
B/f		3,095	
11.12.X1	1201159	797	
17.12.X1	CHQ12045		1,402
28.12.X1	1201262	602	
11.01.X2	0102078	698	
17.01.X2	CHQ10037		1,693
28.01.X2	0102222	717	
08.02.X2	0202089	750	
15.02.X2	CHQ20041		1,399
22.02.X2	0202199	727	
08.03.X2	0302051	699	
15.03.X2	CHQ30042		1,415
22.03.X2	0302198	697	
05.04.X2	0402029	702	
12.04.X2	CHQ40039		1,477
19.04.X2	0402176	741	
03.05.X2	0502023	710	
10.05.X2	CHQ50024		1,396
17.05.X2	0502172	716	
31.05.X2	0502287	634	

chapter 9:
AUDIT OF LIABILITIES (AND RELATED ITEMS)

1   What third party document provides excellent evidence for auditors concerning trade creditors?

2   When might auditors circularise creditors?

3   How will an auditor test completeness of recording of purchases?

4   What three tests will auditors carry out on the balance for accruals?

5   Give two examples of long-term liabilities.

6   What tests should be carried out to determine the completeness of long-term liabilities?

7   You are an audit senior who is going to audit creditors and to reconcile the following purchase ledger balances at 31 December to the suppliers statements summaries given below and on the following pages, using the purchase ledger account details. (The supplier statement summaries have previously been prepared by your audit assistant.)

Wembley Wheels Ltd	15,500
Mitchell's Classic Oils Ltd	5,250
Patel Engine Parts Ltd	27,200
Helga Autoparts Ltd	25,890
Leather Seats Ltd	nil

Task

Set out your objectives, work done, results and conclusions drawn on a working paper including your proposed adjustment to the draft accounts.

3 3 3 3 3

Details of Suppliers statements

Wembley Wheels Ltd 31 Erdington Drive Wembley

Statement at 31 December 20X1 Vat No: 123 4567 98

Payments are due within 30 days

		£	£	£
27	31/10/X1	2,212. 75	387. 25	2,600
28	17/11/X1	6,297. 88	1,102. 12	7,400
31	2/12/X1	4,680. 85	819. 15	5,500
Total now due				15,500

Mitchells Classic Oils Ltd 24 Grove Estate Norwich

Statement at 31 December 20X1 Vat No 123 8668 27

Due for payment 25 January 20X2

		£	£	£
201	8/12/X1	1,319. 15	230. 85	1,550
212	10/12/X1	3,617. 02	632. 98	4,250
215	23/12/X1	851. 06	148. 94	1,000
Total due				6,800

Patel Engine Parts Ltd The Manor Works Grimsby

Statement at 31 December 20X1 Vat No 123 9667 29

Due for payment 31 January 20X2

		£	£	£
1223	13/11/X1	17,361. 70	3,038. 30	20,400
1771	1/12/X1	10,212. 77	1,787. 23	12,000
1812	27/12/X1	4,425. 53	774. 47	5,200
Total due				37,600

Helga Autoparts Ltd 261 Coleshill Rd Luton

Statement at 31 December 20X1 Vat No 123 5678 43

Due for payment 31 January 20X2

		£	£	£
8789	27/10/X1	85. 11	14. 89	100
8838	6/11/X1	6,663. 83	1,166. 17	7,830
8921	8/12/X1	15,285. 11	2,674. 89	17,960
Total due				25,890

Leather Seats Ltd 20 Sarahall Rd Brighton

Statement at 31 December 20X1 Vat No 123 7890 67

Due for payment 31 January 20X2

		£	£	£
12281	11/11/X1	102. 12	17. 88	120
12291	12/11/X1	1,787. 23	312. 77	2,100
12292	1/12/X1	2,553. 19	446. 81	3,000
12297	30/12/X1	3,913. 19	684. 81	4,598
Total due				9,818

Details of Purchase Ledger Accounts

Wembley Wheels Ltd			
Date	**Item**	**DR**	**CR**
		£	£
1/12/X1	Bal b/f		10,000
3/12/X1	Invoice		5,500
31/12/X1	Bal c/f	15,500	

Mitchells Classic Oils Ltd			
Date	**Item**	**DR**	**CR**
		£	£
8/12/X1	Invoice		1,550
10/12/X1	Invoice		4,250
28/12/X1	Invoice		1,000
30/12/X1	Payment	1,550	
31/12/X1	Bal c/f	5,250	

Patel Engine Parts Ltd

Date	Item	DR £	CR £
1/12/X1	Bal b/f		20,400
5/12/X1	Invoice		12,000
28/12/X1	Discount	200	
28/12/X1	Payment	5,000	
31/12/X1	Bal c/f	27,200	

Helga Autoparts Ltd

Date	Item	DR £	CR £
1/12/X1	Bal b/f		7,930
8/12/X1	Invoice		17,960
31/12/X1	Bal c/f	25,890	

Leather Seats Ltd

Date	Item	DR £	CR £
1/12/X1	Bal b/f		2,220
3/12/X1	Invoice		3,000
27/12/X1	Payment	5,220	
31/12/X1	Account settled		

8   Kitchy Kabinets Ltd buys, sells and fits high quality kitchen furniture. Most of its suppliers are traditional craftsmen who do not operate the most efficient billing systems.

Task 1

Set out the objectives of year-end cut off procedures relating to the purchases system of Kitchy Kabinets Ltd.

Task 2

Identify the purchases year-end cut-off tests you would carry out on the audit of Kitchy Kabinets Ltd.

9   You are now going to complete a supplier statement reconciliation at Glad Rags Limited. The necessary information, including the sample you have selected, is given below. Your working paper should set out the objectives of the test, the work done and your conclusions.

Supplier	Balance per purchase ledger £
AA Fabrics Limited	387
Fine Fabrics Limited	102,486
Terry's Threads	97,429
The Fabric Wholesaler	112,462

Supplier statements

FINE FABRICS LIMITED

Unit 12 Marlowe Industrial Park Marlowe	To: Glad Rags Limited The Old Mill Forseby	VAT registration: 012 2345 56

Invoice number	Date		Balance
B/f from October		52,395.72	52,395.72
33147	01.11.X4	12,483.99	64,879.71
33150	04.11.X4	3,499.46	68,379.17
33153	08.11.X4	32,002.17	100,381.34
Receipt – thanks	10.11.X4	(100,381.34)	0.00
33155	11.11.X4	2,878.75	2,878.75
33157	12.11.X4	24,956.83	27,835.58
33158	16.11.X4	23,945.67	51,781.25
33159	18.11.X4	245.99	52,027.24
33161	19.11.X4	4,593.92	56,621.16
33163	23.11.X4	284.55	56,905.71
33169	24.11.X4	27,984.43	84,890.14
33171	25.11.X4	14,938.69	99,828.83
33175	29.11.X4	2,409.18	102,238.01
33177	30.11.X4	248.00	102,486.01

Invoice to:	Glad Rags Limited, The Old Mill, Foresby
Invoice date:	27 November 20X4
Invoice number:	11/04

THE FABRIC WHOLESALER

Invoice	Date	Amount
B/f	Oct	44,658.11
SI1083	01.11.X4	24,472.45
SI1089	05.11.X4	15,163.68
Receipt	10.11.X4	(84,294.24)
SI1092	12.11.X4	28,155.37
SI1094	17.11.X4	13,467.32
SI1097	19.11.X4	37,298.44
SI1101	22.11.X4	32,131.25
SI1103	26.11.X4	1,410.00
		112,462.38

4, The Ridge, Overhill, OV12 8RL
VAT Registration number: 933 9345 925

	Terry's threads 2, Lark Close Garton VAT registration number: 123 9443 35
Balance owed by Glad Rags @ 30 November 20X4: Comprising invoices: 22381, 22384, 22388, 22394, 22396, 22397	100,374.72

AA FABRICS LIMITED Unit 27 Rosehill Industrial Estate Rosehill	VAT registration number: 022 4776 345
Glad Rags Limited Balance at 30 November 20X4 Inv1011 17 Nov 20X4	 386.88

Credit note

	Terry's threads 2, Lark Close Garton VAT registration number: 123 9443 35
Credit to: Glad Rags Limited Date: 27.11.X4 Credit note number: C10254 Re invoice 22384	 2,945.51

10 Clare will be carrying out the work on the creditors figure for Greenfingers Limited, reconciling a sample of supplier statements to the purchases ledger. She has never audited creditors before. Using the purchase ledger listing given below, identify the balances that must be sampled and set out the work that must be carried out on the selected sample.

Purchase ledger list of balances	
Supplier	*Balance at 31.12.20X4*
	£
A1 Plants Limited	2,305
Beautiful Begonias etc Limited	6,478
Dawsons Fencing Limited	75,003
Garden Supplies Limited	5,524
Greek Terracotta Company Limited	7,398
Hardy's Catering Supplies Limited	12,688
Kellers Limited	1,938
Oasis Plant Company Limited	2,895
Oliver Limited	10,355
Seeds Limited	3,748
Trees and Shrubs Limited	8,946
Very Nice Garden Company Limited	89,035
	226,313

11 Set out the work that you will complete on the accruals balance at Greenfingers Limited.

chapter 10:
AUDIT COMPLETION
AND REPORTING

1   Give three examples of post balance sheet events which might necessitate adjusting the financial statements.

2   What are the auditors' duties with regard to subsequent events after the audit report has been signed?

3   What should auditors do if management refuse to sign a letter of representation?

4   What are the basic elements of the standard audit report?

5   When would an auditor issue an adverse opinion?

6   Outline the four possible types of opinion in an audit report where there are matters that affect the auditor's opinion and explain why each would arise.

7   You are an audit senior working on the audit of Butler Buses Ltd. Owing to delays because of the sudden departure of the finance director from the company, the audit has seriously overrun its allotted time, and you are about to be called away on another job, leaving the audit team working for you to complete the audit. Team members have raised a number of queries about various audit completion procedures and you need to answer them before you leave the audit.

    On the last day you are on the audit you have a meeting with the sales director who has taken temporary charge of the accounts department. The sales director has not had recent accountancy experience and wants you to explain the meaning of various terms used in the audit report. He is also unwilling to sign a letter of representation, stating that you should have done sufficient work on the matters covered in the draft letter of representation and should not therefore need to obtain a letter of representation.

    Task 1

    List for your audit team the signs that may indicate that the company may not be able to continue as a going concern.

    Task 2

    List the main procedures that auditors should carry out to determine whether there are any material events after the balance sheet date.

    Task 3

    Explain to the sales director the main purposes of the letter of representation and what will happen if the directors refuse to sign the letter of representation.

8 Jules has calculated some financial statement ratios to see if Glad Rags Limited's financial statements appear to be consistent within themselves (given on the next page). He has not drawn a conclusion as a result of his tests. Draw a conclusion as to whether the ratios indicate whether the financial statements appear to be consistent within themselves, giving reasons for your answer.

The key figures from the profit and loss account are turnover, which is £7,103,495, gross profit £2,121,814 and net profit £680,515.

Client:	Glad Rags Ltd	Prepared by:	J Devoran
Accounting date:	30 November 20X4	Date:	21 January 20X5
		Reviewed by:	
		Date:	

Overall review of financial statements

Objective: To ensure that the financial statements appear to be consistent within t hemselves.

Work done: Financial statement ratios carried out.

Ratios		20X3
$\dfrac{\text{Gross profit}}{\text{Turnover}} \times 100$	$\dfrac{2{,}121{,}814}{7{,}103.495} \times 100 = 29.87\%$	(30.2%)
$\dfrac{\text{Net profit}}{\text{Turnover}} \times 100$	$\dfrac{680{,}515}{7{,}103{,}495} \times 100 = 9.58\%$	(9.52%)
$\dfrac{\text{Debtors}}{\text{Turnover}} \times 365$	$\dfrac{1{,}345{,}933}{7{,}103{,}495} \times 365 = 69$ days	(67 days)
$\dfrac{\text{Creditors}}{\text{Cost of sales}} \times 365$	$\dfrac{365{,}038}{4{,}981{,}681} \times 365 = 27$ days	(28 days)

9 The issue of going concern was raised as a risk of the audit of Glad Rags Limited for the year end 30 November 20X4. Highlight what particular matters you will consider in carrying out your going concern review.

10 You have been reviewing some areas of the audit file that Jules has been completing. Jules is not aware of any audit area where evidence has been restricted to representations from Gladys. In the management representation section of the audit file, he has written 'not applicable'.

Draft a note to Jules, explaining why it will be necessary to draft a management representation letter for Glad Rags, indicating what will be included in that letter.

11 You have now completed the audit work on Glad Rags Limited, and have concluded that an unqualified audit opinion should be given. Draft the relevant opinion paragraph.

12 You have noted from the previous year's audit files for Greenfingers Limited that the company was in breach of some fire regulations relating to fire doors in one of the businesses premises. On enquiry, you have discovered that the company has still not undertaken the remedial work to ensure that fire doors are compliant with the law. You note that your firm discussed the matter with the managing director last year and concluded that the only potential effect of non-compliance was a fine if the premises are inspected, which the directors believed was unlikely.

a) Outline what the impact would be on your audit of a fire inspection after the yearend, resulting in an immaterial fine for the company.

b) Outline what audit work you will do in respect of the non-compliance with the fire regulations if no such visit takes place.

13 You feel that the situation with regard to the fire doors should be confirmed in a management representation letter. Draft the appropriate paragraph of that letter. (You are only required to draft the paragraph relating to the fire doors.)

14 Clare has been asking you about the impact of the situation with the fire doors on the audit opinion for Greenfingers Limited. She has asked you whether, as there is uncertainty whether the company will be charged a fine, the auditors need to refer to this uncertainty in the audit report.

Outline whether the situation with the fire doors will have any impact on the audit report.

15 During the course of the audit work on stock at Greenfingers, a material error was discovered. On 30 December a new recruit left a door to the plant room at one of the stores open overnight which meant that the heat regulation system failed and a large number of plants included in the stock count at the yearend died after the stocktake, and should have been written off. However, these plants have been included in stock at full value (£67,495). The director does not wish to amend the financial statements as he insists that the stock did exist at the yearend and therefore it is fair to present that situation and recognise the loss on the stock in the next financial year.

a) For Clare's benefit, outline briefly why the director is wrong in his opinion.

b) Draft the appropriate opinion paragraph for the audit report (assuming this is the only material problem you have discovered) if the director does not change his mind and amend the financial statements.

PRACTICE SKILLS TEST

EGMUND LTD

Time allowed: 4 hours

SKILLS TEST

COVERAGE OF PERFORMANCE CRITERIA

The following performance criteria are covered in this simulation.

Element	PC Coverage
17.1	**Contribute to the planning of an audit assignment**
	a) Ascertain accounting systems under review and record them clearly on appropriate working papers.
	b) Identify control objectives correctly.
	c) Assess risks accurately.
	d) Record significant weaknesses in control correctly.
	e) Identify account balances to be verified and the associated risks.
	f) Select an appropriate sample.
	g) Select or devise appropriate tests in accordance with the organisation's procedures.
	h) Follow confidentiality and security procedures.
	i) Formulate the proposed audit plan clearly and in consultation with appropriate personnel.
	j) Submit the proposed audit plan to the appropriate person for approval.
17.2	**Contribute to the conduct of an audit assignment**
	a) Conduct tests correctly and as specified in the audit plan, record test results properly and draw valid conclusions from them.
	b) Establish the existence, completeness, ownership, valuation and description of assets and liabilities and gather appropriate evidence to support these findings.
	c) Identify all matters of an unusual nature and refer them promptly to the audit supervisor.
	d) Identify and record material and significant errors, deficiencies or other variations from standard and report them to the audit supervisor.
	e) Examine the IT environment and assess it for security.
	g) Follow confidentiality and security procedures.
17.3	**Prepare related draft reports**
	a) Prepare clear and concise draft reports relating to the audit assignment and submit them for review and approval in line with organisational procedures.
	b) Draw valid conclusions and provide evidence to support them.
	c) Make constructive and practicable recommendations.
	d) Discuss and agree your preliminary conclusions and recommendations with the audit supervisor.
	e) Follow confidentiality and security procedures.

The following performance criteria are not covered in this simulation and should be assessed separately.

17.2 (f) Conduct discussions with staff operating the system to be audited in a manner which promotes professional relationships between auditing and operational staff.

Any missing range statements should also be assessed separately.

DATA AND TASKS

Instructions

This simulation is designed to test your ability to implement audit procedures.

The situation is provided below and permanent information is on page 88.

The tasks you are to complete are set out on pages 84 to 87.

Your answers should be set out in the answer book provided immediately after this assessment, starting on page 105. It is anticipated that sufficient space is provided in the answer book for answers. However, a couple of spare pages are provided at the back of the answer book for use, if necessary.

You are allowed four hours to complete your work.

A high level of accuracy is required. Check your work carefully before handing it in.

Correcting fluid may be used but it should be used in moderation. Errors should be crossed out neatly and clearly. You should write in black ink, not pencil.

You are advised to read the whole of the simulation before commencing as all of the information may be of value and is not necessarily supplied in the sequence in which you might wish to deal with it. The simulation contains a large volume of data which you may need in order to complete the tasks. An indication of the time allowed for each task is given for further guidance and the amount of space allowed in the answer booklet should be indicative of the length of responses expected and allows for candidates with larger writing.

THE SITUATION

Egmund Limited is a private limited company which runs an egg farm situated in rural Hertfordshire.

The company's auditors are A Byrdez and Associates, practising from offices in Knebworth. You are the senior in charge of the audit and you have an audit junior, Delsia Deans. Your audit team is carrying out the audit for the year ended 30 September 20X7.

The audit manager, Wanda Wing, has held a meeting with the client, and now has several tasks which she would like you to complete. These are set out on pages 84 to 87.

TASKS TO BE COMPLETED

Task 1

a) Explain what you understand by a control environment and what particular factors should be looked at in assessing the control environment of a company. Use the space provided on page 106 of your answer book to record your response.

b) Review the permanent information provided on pages 88 to 92 and prepare an assessment of Egmund Limited's control environment, taking into consideration the factors you have identified in part (a) above. Write your answer on page 108 of your answer book.

(Allow 25 minutes for this task)

Task 2

a) Explain what you understand by inherent risk in relation to a client as a whole. Discuss the particular factors you would take into consideration in assessing an entity's inherent risk. Record your response on page 109 of your answer book.

b) Review the permanent information provided on pages 88 to 92 and prepare an assessment of inherent risk at the overall financial statement level in respect of Egmund Limited. Use the factors you have identified in part (a) above. Note your assessment on page 111 of your answer book.

c) List the factors which might affect inherent risk in individual account balances or transactions. Use the space provided on page 112 of your answer book.

(Allow 20 minutes for this task)

Task 3

Assurance is the basis for a judgement that undetected material error does not exist.

One of the requirements of a standard audit report is for external auditors to state they have obtained sufficient evidence to give reasonable assurance that the financial statements are free from material misstatement.

Auditors gain the reasonable assurance they require from three sources, one of which is inherent assurance (as covered in Task 2, part (c) above).

a) State the two other sources from which an external auditor would gain the necessary audit assurance in respect of a financial statement assertion. Use the space provided on page 113 of your answer book to record your response.

b) List the financial statement assertions. Use page 114 of your answer book for this.

c) Explain what is meant by the term test of control. Use the space on page 114 of your answer book.

d)   Explain what is meant by the term substantive procedure. Do this on page 115 of your answer book.

(Allow 20 minutes for this task)

Task 4

Delsia Deans, the audit junior is on her first job and does not understand the concept of materiality. Draft an e-mail message to Delsia, explaining what this means. Use the space provided on page 117 of the answer book to draft your e-mail.

(Allow 10 minutes for this task)

Task 5

Your manager has decided that a sample size of 10 should be used for the confirmation of trade debtors. Review the debtors listing on page 93 and select which balances should be circularised. Set out your answer on the headed paper on page 119 of your answer book, and give the basis for your selection.

(Allow 10 minutes for this task)

Task 6

You are still doing your debtors circularisation. A few weeks ago you sent out confirmation requests to 10 debtors (all the debtors in your sample). Six replies have been received and these are on pages 94 to 96.

You should use the confirmation replies and debtors listing along with the documents listed below.

- credit note reserve (page 97)
- bad debt provision (page 97)
- cash book receipts (page 97)
- sales ledger account (page 98)
- sales invoice (page 98)

Use the headed paper on pages 120 and 121 in your answer book to set out the objectives of the test, the work done, the results and the conclusion. Your conclusion should include some consideration of the work to be done on the debtors from whom no reply was received.

(Allow 35 minutes for this task)

Task 7

Consider a typical purchases system. Identify what are its control objectives at each stage from order to payment and list the typical internal controls that would be used to achieve such control objectives.

Use the pro-forma provided on page 122 of your answer book to record your answer.

(Allow 20 minutes for this task)

Task 8

Identify the control weaknesses in Egmund Limited's procedures for ordering, receiving and payment for supplies. Use page 123 of your answer book to record your answer.

(Allow 20 minutes for this task)

Task 9

On page 99 to 104 of this assessment, you will see six of the invoices supporting the sample selected from the cheque payments for the year.

Draw up an audit plan to verify the validity and accuracy of these payments. Do this on page 124 of your answer book.

(Allow 20 minutes for this task)

Task 10

Egmund Limited does not maintain a creditors ledger. Review the purchases and payments cashbook systems to determine how the company might identify trade creditors at the end of its financial year. (Include expenditure items such as telephone and electricity, but not any accruals or prepayments of part invoices.) Use the schedule on page 125 of the answer book.

(Allow 10 minutes for this task)

Task 11

The company does not have any detailed stock records or internal controls over stocks of eggs and fresh oven-ready chickens.

a)   Assess whether this constitutes a lack of proper accounting records.

b)   State what factors should be taken into consideration in deciding on the level of internal control that should be exercised over stocks of eggs and fresh chickens, given the corporate culture of flexibility, teamwork and efficiency that the Hennmans intend to maintain within Egmund Limited.

c)   Design a substantive analytical procedure to confirm the completeness of egg sales using factors such as the number of laying hens, their egg output and so on.

d)   Draft a management letter point setting out your recommendations regarding internal controls over the accounting for egg and fresh chicken stocks.

Record your responses to the above in the space provided on page 126 and 127 of your answer book.

(Allow 25 minutes for this task)

Task 12

List the control objectives of a payroll system in the space provided on page 128 of your answer book.

(Allow 5 minutes for this task)

Task 13

During your work on debtors it was established that the debt from Patel Pastries was unlikely to be recovered and that Egmund Limited has no security for this debt. However, the client refuses to adjust the accounts to reflect this. It is your opinion that this will have a material effect on the financial statements, but will not render them totally misleading. Your manager has asked you to draft an appropriate opinion paragraph for the audit report. Set this out on the headed paper on page 129 of your answer book.

(Allow 10 minutes for this task)

Task 14

Delsia Deans is working on the payroll. You were both invited out to lunch with the client and Delsia left her desk with all of the files she has been working on still open.

Delsia has got behind with her work and she has suggested taking some work home to catch up.

You have spoken to her about the above two matters, but your manager Wanda Wing has asked you to write a memo to Delsia confirming your discussions. Use the memo paper on page 130 of your answer book.

(Allow 10 minutes for this task)

Client	Egmund Ltd
Accounting date	30 September 20X7

Prepared by	AAS
Date	XX/XX/XX
Reviewed by	WW
Date	XX/XX/XX

PERMANENT INFORMATION

Understanding the business entity

Egmund Limited is a private limited company whose principal activity is the production and sale of eggs. It has been in operation for 6 years and runs a farm in Hertfordshire.

Shareholders: Harry Hennman (50%)
                   Joyti Hennman (50%) – Harry's wife

Directors: Harry Hennman
                   Joyti Hennman

Joyti used to own a hair salon and Harry gained a geography degree, before their venture into egg farming.

The farm manager is Shelly Ovalton who has a BSc in agriculture.

The company sells its eggs to local businesses such as hotels, bakeries, shops and restaurants and some through the farm shop on the premises.

Egmund Limited maintains approximately 5,000 laying hens on a free range basis. Each hen produces approximately one egg a day for about a year, after which the level of production drops off and the eggs become smaller. When this stage is reached, the old hens are replaced by new hens, bred from eggs fertilised at Egmund Limited. The retired hens are slaughtered and sold off at the farm shop on the premises.

Egmund Limited believes in running a lean and efficient operation and has a full time farm manager, plus nine farm assistants, many of whom have been with the company since its inception. The company believes in staff flexibility and the assistants do not have fixed job descriptions. They are expected to be 'part of the team' and 'muck in' to whatever tasks need to be done, eg feeding the hens, cleaning pens, general maintenance, collecting eggs, making up orders, helping with deliveries to commercial customers and serving in the farm shop.

Egmund Limited believes that it can keep the staff head count down by team working, job flexibility and the avoidance of excessive separation of responsibilities. The directors want to keep the company effectively as a family business and every Friday night staff join the directors at the farm house for drinks and snacks.

The Hennmans operate an open door policy to maintain communication with staff and thereby 'keep their finger on the pulse' of what is going on in the business. Staff are encouraged to bring any problems or suggestions to their notice.

Client	Egmund Ltd		Prepared by	AAS
Accounting date	30 September 20X7		Date	XX/XX/XX
			Reviewed by	WW
			Date	XX/XX/XX

The farm functions from the following locations:

- **The farmyard** where the hens are maintained on a free-range basis

- **The farm shop** which sells fresh eggs, fresh chicken, cakes and custard made from surplus or damaged eggs. There is a small kitchen at the rear of the shop where the baking and custard making are done.

- **The barn**. This serves a variety of operational purposes:

    - housing of chickens when poor weather conditions prevail

    - making up orders of eggs for delivery to commercial customers or packaging them for sale in the farm shop

    - preparation for sale of fresh chickens

    - storage of feedstuffs and farm equipment.

- **Farmhouse study/office**. This in effect serves as the administrative nerve centre of the business where the Hennmans keep the computer and the accounting records.

ACCOUNTING SYSTEMS

Computer environment

A standard software package is used for the accounting records.

The systems are password protected so that only those with authority can enter the system. There are backup procedures in place, but Joyti admits that sometimes she forgets to do this.

The directors have not considered what they would do should any of the systems fail.

Management accounts

Management accounts are produced each month in the form of a profit and loss account and balance sheet. The profit and loss account is analysed between commercial sales and farm shop sales.

The directors review and discuss the management accounts each month, and any unusual or unexpected results are investigated.

The Hennmans rely heavily on the management accounts to control the business on a top-down basis. They believe that the business is not complex and they have a good idea of how many eggs and chickens they should have sold and what their income and profitability should be.

Client	Egmund Ltd
Accounting date	30 September 20X7

Prepared by	AAS
Date	XX/XX/XX
Reviewed by	WW
Date	XX/XX/XX

At the end of each quarter the Hennmans sit down with Shelly the farm manager to discuss the performance shown by the accounts, any problems arising and sharing ideas for the next quarter. During the meeting, Shelly presents the Hennmans with an Excel chart showing daily egg production.

Sales and debtors

Sales to commercial businesses are made on a credit basis. However, sales from the farm shop are done on a cash only basis.

Orders from commercial businesses are taken over the telephone by a farm assistant in the farm shop. These are recorded in a standard duplicate order book of the type obtainable from a newsagent or stationery shop. (The company finds this type of stationery very practical and cost effective.) The top copy is taken over to the barn so that the order can be fulfilled.

When delivery is made, a three part pre-numbered despatch note is prepared by a farm assistant. The copies are distributed as follows:

- Top copy sent with the eggs to the customer. The customer signs this to acknowledge due receipt of the eggs in good condition. On return, these signed copies are filed in a 'proof of delivery' file in the barn.

- Second copy is taken over to the farm office to one of the Hennmans for invoicing using the invoicing facility on the computer. The invoice is posted to the sales ledger and nominal ledger. The sales invoice is produced in two parts:

  - sent to customer
  - stapled to delivery note and filed in numerical order.

- Third copy. This remains in the order book.

A monthly sales ledger control account is produced by the computer and the balance is agreed to the total of sales ledger balances printout.

Joyti manages the credit control function:

- Credit references are taken out for all new customers
- A letter is sent if an invoice is outstanding for more than 30 days
- After a further 14 days, a telephone call is made
- After 90 days, the debt is handed over to solicitors to institute court proceeding to recover the amount owed

Joyti expects the bad debts figure to be around 5% of total debtors.

There is no cash register in the farm shop. The sales cash is kept in a locked box. No invoices are issued. There is a small cash float of £20.

Client	Egmund Ltd		Prepared by	AAS
Accounting date	30 September 20X7		Date	XX/XX/XX
			Reviewed by	WW
			Date	XX/XX/XX

Receipting and banking

Banking is done on a daily basis by either Harry or Joyti.

At the end of each day, money from the farm shop is cashed up by Shelly, the farm manager, who uses a standard per carbon book, to record the total takings. The top copy showing the amount of sales cash for the day is handed to one of the Hennmans and the carbon copy remains in the book, which is also kept in the cash box in the farm shop. Overnight the cash box, including the £20 float, is hidden under the counter where it is not visible to potential burglars.

Joyti enters each debtor's cheque remittance into the debtors ledger computer system via the receipts screen. Prior to lodgement the debtors' cheques are listed onto a bank paying-in slip plus the farm shop cash takings. The company banks all its remittances on a daily basis.

The actual banking is usually done by Harry or Joyti, but sometimes when they are busy, the farm manager Shelly goes to the bank. For security reasons, they vary the times that the banking is carried out.

Stock

The company has minimal stocks comprising mainly feedstuffs for the hens.

The eggs are collected early each morning by the farm assistants, who know what to do and get on with the task. The eggs are taken to the barn where they are cleaned up before being sorted into size and then put into containers pending delivery/sale to customers. This comprises either cardboard boxes of six eggs or trays of three dozen.

Approximately 50 hens are retired, slaughtered and sold each week. Demand for these fresh birds is fierce and the company tends not to hold any stocks overnight.

No stock records are maintained and the farm manager keeps an eye on things. Harry and Joyti tend to use a top-down approach to controlling the cost of feedstuffs. They do this by monitoring the expenditure levels shown in the monthly management accounts.

Purchases and payments

The farm manager Shelly is respnsible for placing all orders relating to farm operations other than for fixed assets. Only Harry and Joyti may place orders for capital expenditure.

Orders are made out in duplicate:

- Top copy is sent to the supplier
- Second copy is held in a file pending receipt of the delivery
- Third copy remains bound in the order book

All deliveries have to be made to the barn. When goods arrive, the farm manager Shelly checks them against the delivery note and the order. She also ensures that there is no damage and the quality of the goods received is appropriate. She ticks off the items on the delivery note but does not sign it in any manner.

Sometimes, when Shelly is not around, or is very busy, one of the farm assistants might carry out the checking of goods received.

When the supplier's invoice is received, Shelly applies a rubber stamp, as below:

Order Number	
Delivery checked	
Ledger code	
Payment approved	
Cheque number	
Date	

Shelly completes the first four boxes on the stamped grid, staples the invoice together with the delivery note and order and passes these over to the farm office for payment.

Egmund Ltd does not maintain a purchases ledger as normally suppliers' invoices are settled on a 30 days basis. Unpaid invoices are kept in one file and when these are paid, the cheque number and date are filled into the grid on the invoice and it is then transferred to a paid invoices file.

Some expenses such as petrol, telephone, electricity and vets fees do not go through the ordering system. Instead these invoices, when received, go straight into the unpaid invoices files.

Cheques paid are processed into the computerised payments cash book. Bank charges and bounced cheques shown on the bank statements are also processed into the payments cash book.

At the end of each month Harry performs the following tasks:

- Prepare a monthly bank reconciliation
- Prepare a schedule of creditors using the unpaid invoices file

The authorised cheque signatories are Harry and Joyti Hennman, though in practice it is usually Joyti that prepares and signs the cheques.

Payroll

This is prepared by Joyti using the computer.

The payroll is reviewed by Harry to identify any unusual amounts.

Egmund Ltd
Aged debtors at 30 September 20X7

A/C no.	Customer	Balance £	Current £	30 days £	60 days £	90 days £	>90 days £
1	Ahmed Ltd	234	234				
2	Anchor and Chain	2,413	1,051	989	373		
3	Amber Hector	347	340			7	
4	Avocado and Orange	1,098	261	175	312	350	
5	Bakers Dozen	234	234				
6	Bakit Ltd	1,125	457	499	169		
7	Beehive	987	595	392			
8	Cafe Rio	250	150	100			
9	Cahoot2	365	365				
10	Cakes U Like	1,275	768	560			(53)
11	Chopstix	1,918	986	765	166		
12	Daljits Delights	1,496	865	631			
13	Delias Den	178	178				
14	Dog and Duck	58		58			
15	Dudek Donut	39		39			
16	Eatons	254	150	104			
17	East and West Cafe	45	45				
18	Emma's Teas	120	120				
19	Funtastic	425	125	150	150		
20	Fruit and Food	54	54				
21	Gateau X	476	369	107			
22	Giluame and Co	134		134			
23	Goat and Hare	98	50		48		
24	Halina	103	103				
25	Heartbreak Hotel	1,257	693	564			
26	Honeybunn and Son	1,699	545	640	414	100	
27	Hunky Dory	42	42				
28	Igor Biscuits	1,835			750	595	490
29	Jam Tarts	75	75				
30	Junkets	127	127				
31	Laddets	513	350		163		
32	Leroy Lemon	100	100				
33	Leungs	1,089	555	559		(25)	
34	Nice Nosh	145		145			
35	Patel Pastries	2,475	1,056	589	555	275	
36	Pie in Sky	2,109	998	786	325		
37	Ping Ann	697	345	352			
38	Raymondos	98	98				
39	Sunjeev Snacks	57	57				
		26,044	12,541	8,338	3,425	1,295	437

Debtors circularisation replies

Auditors
Gigg Lane
Knebworth
Hertfordshire

Dear Sirs

.... EGMUND ....Limited

We confirm that, except as noted below, the balance of £..2,413............

was owing by us to the above company at ....30/09/X7..............

Name of business ....ANCHOR AND CHAIN..............

Signed ....A J Riley..............

Position held ....Accounts Manager..............

Date ....12/12/X7..............

Payment of £450 on 28/09/X7

Auditors
Gigg Lane
Knebworth
Hertfordshire

Dear Sirs

.... EGMUND ....Limited

We confirm that, except as noted below, the balance of £..1,125............

was owing by us to the above company at ....30/09/X7..............

Name of business ....BAKIT LTD..............

Signed ....B Walsh..............

Position held ....Head of Accounts..............

Date ....16/12/X7..............

Goods returned 20 September 20X7 – £50
(included on invoice 5984)

Debtors circularisation replies (continued)

Auditors
Gigg Lane
Knebworth
Hertfordshire

Dear Sirs

................EGMUND................Limited

We confirm that, except as noted below, the balance of £...1,918.............

was owing by us to the above company at ....30/09/X7.............

Name of business ....CHOPSTIX.............

Signed ....U R Wright.............

Position held ....Manager.............

Date ....20/12/X7.............

Disputed invoice number 4848 (£120) – 18/08/X7 –
eggs not very fresh

Auditors
Gigg Lane
Knebworth
Hertfordshire

Dear Sirs

................EGMUND................Limited

We confirm that, except as noted below, the balance of £...1,699.............

was owing by us to the above company at ....30/09/X7.............

Name of business ....HONEYBUNN AND SON.............

Signed ....B Hyde.............

Position held ....S/L Controller.............

Date ....20/12/X7.............

Invoice no. 492 contains transposition error – total is for
£51 but should be £15, ie overcharged by £36.

Debtors circularisation replies (continued)

Auditors
Gigg Lane
Knebworth
Hertfordshire

Dear Sirs

...............**EGMUND**...................Limited

We confirm that, except as noted below, the balance of £...1,835...........

was owing by us to the above company at ....30/09/X7.............

Name of business ....IGOR BISCUITS.....................

Signed ....*Carlos Kyckov*.....................

Position held ....*Accounts Supervisor*.....................

Date ....*24/12/X7*.....................

    AGREED

Auditors
Gigg Lane
Knebworth
Hertfordshire

Dear Sirs

...............**EGMUND**...................Limited

We confirm that, except as noted below, the balance of £...2,109...........

was owing by us to the above company at ....30/09/X7.............

Name of business ....PIE IN SKY.....................

Signed ....*Mary Ross*.....................

Position held ....*S/L*.....................

Date ....*02/12/X7*.....................

    Cheque paid 06/10/X7 – £325

Credit note reserve

(credit notes issued after the year end relating to sales before the year end)

	Invoice no.	£
Funtastic	4812	22
Goat and Hare	4865	48
Ping Ann	5763	5
Bakit	5984	50
Cahoot 2	6345	15
		140

Bad debt provision

	£
Laddets	163
Sunjeev Snacks	57
Amber Hector	7
Hunky Dory	42
Chopstix	120
	389

Cash book receipts

October 20X7 Sales Ledger Receipts (Extract)

Date	Description	£
2	Halina	103
2	Ahmed Ltd	450
2	Goat and Hare	50
5	Jam Tarts	75
5	Leroy Lemon	50
5	Raymondos	98
6	Pie in Sky	325
6	Gateau X	107
7	Dudek Donut	39

Sales ledger account
Honeybunn and Son – 30 September 20X7

Date	Invoice no.	Debit	Credit	Balance
b/f				672
2/5	3507	147		819
18/5	3992	102		922
1/6	Receipt		150	772
1/6	4507	44		816
16/6	4778	56		872
5/7	Receipt		347	525
10/7	4927	414		939
1/8	Receipt		175	764
2/8	5511	135		899
15/8	5742	270		1,169
28/8	5810	235		1,404
7/9	Receipt		250	1,154
12/9	6187	300		1,454
15/9	6291	245		1,699

Note: See invoice 4778 below.

SALES INVOICE
EGMUND LIMITED
POULTRY GRANGE FARM
HERTFORDSHIRE
HP10 8HN
'EXCELLENCE IN EGGS'

To: Honeybunn and Son
Sunny Gardens
Harpendon
Herts

Sales invoice no. 4778
Order no. 199876
Date: 10 July 20X7

Quantity	Description	Unit price	•
51	Large brown	1.00	51

should be 15

| Payment due in 30 days | Total due | | •51 |

1047

CHICKEN FEEDS LTD
KINGS LANGLEY
0293 661402

20 March 20X7

Egmund Ltd
Poultry Grange Farm
Hertfordshire
HP10 8HN

	£
20 bags wheat grains	100.00
5 bags roasted soyabeans	20.00
5 bags fish meal	25.00
2 bags nutri-balancer	20.00
10 bags barley	55.00
	220.00

RECEIVED

Order no.	
Delivery checked	0342
Ledger code	Shelly
Payment approved	Feeds
Cheque no.	Shelly
Date	10476
	18/03/X7

VAT No. 3 719 846 6

Gold Star Fencing

Accounts receivable
48, Grove Road
Hatfield
0312 489 273

Egmund Ltd
Poultry Grange Farm
Hertfordshire
HP10 8HN

INVOICE NUMBER

113479116

Date	Account no.	Transport	Terms
31.01.X7	W007		30 DAYS NET

Description	Amount
60 6ft fence posts	250.00
Vat @17.5%	43.75
Amount due	293.75

RECEIVED

Order no.	0194
Delivery checked	Nisha
Ledger code	Maintenances
Payment approved	Shelly
Cheque no.	10218
Date	25/02/X7

Reg office 48, Dunstable Rd, Newmarket Reg No 113459118

SALES INVOICE

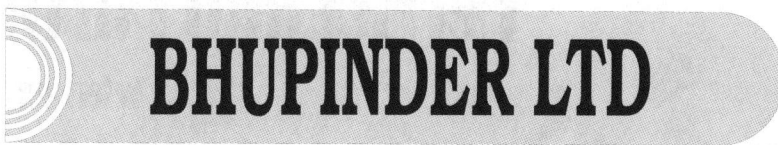

BHUPINDER LTD

74 Cranleigh Mews, Welwyn Garden, S10 9BQ 01693 71592

To:
EGMUND LTD
POULTRY GRANGE FARM
HERTFORDSHIRE

Date: 11.06.X7

Terms: 7 DAYS NET

DESCRIPTION	QUANTITY	AMOUNT
Bugsaway disinfectant	40 litres	288.00
Superkleen detergent	30 litres	234.00
		522.00
VAT	17.5%	91.35
		613.35

RECEIVED

Order no.	
Delivery checked	0615
Ledger code	Shelly
Payment approved	Clean mats
Cheque no.	Shelly
Date	10762
	09/07/X7

REG NO   7499188

VAT NO   0119 469823

Herriot and Partners

Veterinary Clinic

86 Noble Lane
Sunny Ridge
Hertfordshire
S18 5BW

FEE NOTE

£

Anti avian flu treatment of   250
poultry flock on 20/08/X7

RECEIVED

Order no.	0802
Delivery checked	Joyti
Ledger code	Vet fees
Payment approved	Joyti
Cheque no.	10824
Date	17/08/X7

Partners: J Herriot, B.Vet (Hons) RCVP, T Farnon M.V. Ch. B, S Gupta, B Vet, RCVS

Delivery To:

Egmund Ltd
Poultry Grange Farm
Hertfordshire
HP10 8HP

Invoice To:

As above

JIANG

JIANG HARDWARE SUPPLIES
64 HIGH STREET
HARPENDEN
HP75 4JH
061 887 400

INVOICE NO
R104793

Date	Carriage	Terms
18 April 20X7		30 DAYS NET

Description	Price	Amount
20,000 1" Nails	£10.00/1000	20.00
10,000 2" Nails	£12.00/1000	12.00
5,000 brackets	£0.25 each	125.00
		157.00
VAT @ 17.5%		27.47
		184.47

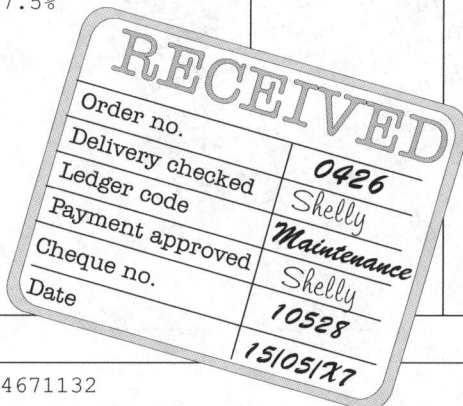

RECEIVED

Order no.	0426
Delivery checked	Shelly
Ledger code	Maintenance
Payment approved	Shelly
Cheque no.	10528
Date	15/05/X7

Reg No 4671132   VAT No 3149827

The Paper Chain

Reg No : 31 74118
VAT No : 7 189 737 4

Date: 29 August 20X7

Invoice No: 4732

Our ref: W147

Stationery House
Stevenage
Hertfordshire
ST3 8BQ
Tel: 091 429 317

To:		
	6 reams A4 Paper	36.00
	VAT at 17½%	6.30
	Amount due	42.30

RECEIVED

Order no.	0828
Delivery checked	Harry
Ledger code	Stationery
Payment approved	Joyti
Cheque no.	10886
Date	26/09/X7

PRACTICE SKILLS TEST

UNIT 17
ANSWER BOOKLET

ANSWER BOOKLET

Task 1

Client	Egmund Ltd
Accounting date	30 September 20X7

Prepared by	A Student
Date	XX/XX/XX
Reviewed by	
Date	

a)   **Control environment**

Task 1 (continued)

Client	Egmund Ltd
Accounting date	30 September 20X7

Prepared by	A Student
Date	XX/XX/XX
Reviewed by	
Date	

Task 1 (continued)

Client	Egmund Ltd
Accounting date	30 September 20X7

Prepared by	A Student
Date	XX/XX/XX
Reviewed by	
Date	

b) **Assessment of control environment**

_____

_____

_____

_____

_____

_____

_____

_____

_____

_____

_____

_____

_____

_____

_____

_____

_____

_____

_____

_____

_____

_____

_____

_____

Task 2

Client	Egmund Ltd
Accounting date	30 September 20X7

Prepared by	A Student
Date	XX/XX/XX
Reviewed by	
Date	

a)   **Inherent risk**

Task 2 (continued)

Client	Egmund Ltd
Accounting date	30 September 20X7

Prepared by	A Student
Date	XX/XX/XX
Reviewed by	
Date	

Task 2 (continued)

Client	Egmund Ltd
Accounting date	30 September 20X7

Prepared by	A Student
Date	XX/XX/XX
Reviewed by	
Date	

b)   **Assessment of inherent risk**

Task 2 (continued)

Client	Egmund Ltd
Accounting date	30 September 20X7

Prepared by	A Student
Date	XX/XX/XX
Reviewed by	
Date	

c)   **Factors which might affect inherent risk in individual account balances or transactions**

Task 3

Client	Egmund Ltd
Accounting date	30 September 20X7

Prepared by	A Student
Date	XX/XX/XX
Reviewed by	
Date	

a)   **Sources of audit assurance**

Task 3 (continued)

Client	Egmund Ltd
Accounting date	30 September 20X7

Prepared by	A Student
Date	XX/XX/XX
Reviewed by	
Date	

b) **Financial statement assertions**

i)

ii)

iii)

iv)

v)

vi)

vii)

viii)

c) **Tests of controls**

Task 3 (continued)

Client	Egmund Ltd
Accounting date	30 September 20X7

Prepared by	A Student
Date	XX/XX/XX
Reviewed by	
Date	

d)   **Substantive procedures**

Task 3 (continued)

Client	Egmund Ltd
Accounting date	30 September 20X7

Prepared by	A Student
Date	XX/XX/XX
Reviewed by	
Date	

Task 4

E-MAIL MESSAGE

To:	**Delsia Deans**
From:	**A Student**
Subject:	**Materiality**

_____

_____

_____

_____

_____

_____

_____

_____

_____

_____

_____

_____

_____

_____

_____

_____

_____

_____

_____

_____

_____

_____

_____

_____

_____

Task 4 (continued)

Task 5

Client	Egmund Ltd
Accounting date	30 September 20X7

Prepared by	A Student
Date	XX/XX/XX
Reviewed by	
Date	

Debtors circularisation sample

Basis of selection

_____

_____

_____

_____

_____

_____

_____

Sample selected

_____

_____

_____

_____

_____

_____

_____

_____

_____

_____

_____

Task 6

Client	Egmund Ltd
Accounting date	30 September 20X7

Prepared by	A Student
Date	XX/XX/XX
Reviewed by	
Date	

Debtors circularisation

Objective

_____

_____

_____

_____

_____

_____

_____

_____

Work done

_____

_____

_____

_____

_____

_____

_____

_____

_____

_____

_____

_____

Task 6 (continued)

Client	Egmund Ltd
Accounting date	30 September 20X7

Prepared by	A Student
Date	XX/XX/XX
Reviewed by	
Date	

Results

_____

_____

_____

_____

_____

_____

_____

_____

_____

_____

_____

_____

_____

_____

_____

Conclusion

_____

_____

_____

_____

_____

_____

Task 7

Client	Egmund Ltd
Accounting date	30 September 20X7

Prepared by	A Student
Date	XX/XX/XX
Reviewed by	
Date	

Stage	Control objectives	Internal controls
1 Ordering		
2 Goods received		
3 Invoice checking and authorisation		
4 Payment		

Task 8

Client	Egmund Ltd
Accounting date	30 September 20X7

Prepared by	A Student
Date	XX/XX/XX
Reviewed by	
Date	

Internal control weaknesses in purchases and payments system

Task 9

Client	Egmund Ltd
Accounting date	30 September 20X7

Prepared by	A Student
Date	XX/XX/XX
Reviewed by	
Date	

Purchases and payments substantive tests of detail

Task 10

Client	Egmund Ltd
Accounting date	30 September 20X7

Prepared by	A Student
Date	XX/XX/XX
Reviewed by	
Date	

Identifying year end creditors

Task 11

Client	Egmund Ltd
Accounting date	30 September 20X7

Prepared by	A Student
Date	XX/XX/XX
Reviewed by	
Date	

Stocks of eggs and fresh chickens

Task 11 (continued)

Client	Egmund Ltd
Accounting date	30 September 20X7

Prepared by	A Student
Date	XX/XX/XX
Reviewed by	
Date	

Task 12

Client	Egmund Ltd
Accounting date	30 September 20X7

Prepared by	A Student
Date	XX/XX/XX
Reviewed by	
Date	

Payroll system control objectives

_____

_____

_____

_____

_____

_____

_____

_____

_____

_____

_____

_____

_____

_____

_____

_____

_____

_____

_____

_____

_____

_____

_____

Task 13

Client	Egmund Ltd
Accounting date	30 September 20X7

Prepared by	A Student
Date	XX/XX/XX
Reviewed by	
Date	

Audit report opinion paragraph

Task 14

Client	Egmund Ltd
Accounting date	30 September 20X7

Prepared by	A Student
Date	XX/XX/XX
Reviewed by	
Date	

MEMO

To: **Delsia Deans**

From: **A Student**

Date: **XX/XX/XX**

Subject: **Confidentiality and safe custody of working papers**

Task 14 (continued)

Client	Egmund Ltd
Accounting date	30 September 20X7

Prepared by	A Student
Date	XX/XX/XX
Reviewed by	
Date	

_____

_____

_____

_____

_____

_____

_____

_____

_____

_____

_____

_____

_____

_____

_____

_____

_____

_____

_____

_____

_____

_____

_____

_____

_____

_____

_____

_____

AAT SPECIMEN SKILLS TEST

DJs LTD

Time allowed: 4 hours

SKILLS TEST

REVISED STANDARDS
TECHNICIAN STAGE
NVQ/SVQ IN ACCOUNTING LEVEL 4
SPECIMEN SIMULATION

AAT

ASSOCIATION
OF ACCOUNTING
TECHNICIANS

SIMULATION—SPECIMEN

IMPLEMENTING AUDITING PROCEDURES

DATA AND TASKS

TO BE COMPLETED BY CANDIDATE

Candidate Name

Registration Number

AAC Code

I confirm that I have received in addition to this booklet an answer booklet for
implementing auditing procedures and that I have access to a calculator.

Signed

Date

Note to assessor:
This booklet must remain sealed until the time of the assessments. If the
assessment is being attempted by separate groups at different times, the
unused booklets must be stored securely until the time of the later
assessment.

Note to candidate:
This booklet must be returned to your assessor with your answer booklet.
After marking, the outer sheet should be removed and placed in your
portfolio.

© AAT 2003
154 Clerkenwell Road, London EC1R 5AD   Tel: +44 (0)20 7837 8600   Fax: +44 (0)20 7837 6970

SIMULATION

COVERAGE OF PERFORMANCE CRITERIA AND RANGE STATEMENTS

The following performance criteria are covered in this simulation.

Element	PC Coverage
17.1	**Contribute to the planning of an audit assignment**
(a)	Ascertain **accounting systems** under review and record them clearly on appropriate working papers.
(b)	Identify control objectives correctly.
(c)	Assess risks accurately.
(d)	Record significant weaknesses in control correctly.
(e)	Identify account balances to be verified and the associated risks.
(f)	Select an appropriate sample.
(g)	Select or devise appropriate **tests** in accordance with the organisation's procedures.
(h)	Follow confidentiality and security procedures.
(i)	Formulate the proposed audit plan clearly and in consultation with appropriate personnel.
(j)	Submit the proposed audit plan to the appropriate person for approval.
17.2	**Contribute to the conduct of an audit assignment**
(a)	Conduct **tests** correctly and as specified in the audit plan, record test results properly and draw valid conclusions from them.
(b)	Establish the existence, completeness, ownership, valuation and description of assets and liabilities and gather appropriate evidence to support these findings.
(c)	Identify all matters of an unusual nature and refer them promptly to the audit supervisor.
(d)	Identity and record material and significant errors, deficiencies or other variations from standard and report them to the audit supervisor.
(e)	Examine the IT environment and assess it for security.
(g)	Follow confidentiality and security procedures.
17.3	**Prepare related draft reports**
(a)	Prepare clear concise **draft reports** relating to the audit assignment and submit them for review and approval in line with organisational procedures.
(b)	Draw valid conclusions and provide evidence to support them.
(c)	Make constructive and practicable recommendations.
(d)	Discuss and agree your preliminary conclusions and recommendations with the audit supervisor.
(e)	Follow confidentiality and security procedures.

The following performance criteria are not covered in this simulation and should be assessed separately.

17.2(f)　　Conduct discussions with staff operating the system to be audited in a manner which promotes professional relationships between auditing and operational staff.

Any missing range statements should be also be assessed separately.

2

ASSOCIATION OF ACCOUNTING TECHNICIANS

DATA AND TASKS

INSTRUCTIONS

This simulation is designed to let you show your ability to implement auditing procedures.

You should read the whole simulation before you start work, so that you are fully aware of you will have to do.

You are allowed **four hours** to complete your work.

Write your answers in the answer booklet provided. Use a blue or black pen, not pencil. If you need more paper for your answers, ask the person in charge.

You may pull apart and rearrange your booklets if you wish to do so, but you must put them back in their original order before handing them in.

You may use correcting fluid, but in moderation. You should cross out your errors neatly and clearly.

Your work must be accurate, so check your work carefully before handing it in.

You are not allowed to refer to any unauthorised material, such as books or notes, while you are working on the simulation. If you have any such material with you, you must hand it to the person in charge before you start work.

Any instances of misconduct will be reported to the AAT, and disciplinary action may be taken.

Coverage of performance criteria and range statements

It is not always possible to cover all performance criteria and range statements in a single simulation. Any performance criteria and range statements not covered must be assessed by other means by the assessor before a candidate can be considered competent.

Performance criteria and range statement coverage for this simulation is shown on page 2.

3

THE SITUATION

You are employed as an audit senior by a firm of accountants and registered auditors. You are helping with the audit of DJs Ltd, a private company which owns a large restaurant complex on the East Coast of England. The year end is 31 December 2002.

The tasks that your manager would like you to complete are set out on pages 5-7 of this booklet.

4

THE TASKS TO BE COMPLETED

Task 1

It has been decided that the audit will concentrate on the following areas:

- sales;
- purchases and creditors;
- payroll;
- fixed assets.

• Read the background information on page 8 of this booklet and for each of the above areas explain why you think they should have been selected for particular attention. Use pages 2-3 of the answer booklet.

Note: consider inherent risk only; do not refer to accounting systems at this stage.

Allow 20 minutes for this task.

Task 2

Review the accounting systems notes on pages 9-10 of this booklet.

• Using the table on pages 4-5 of the answer booklet, set out four weaknesses that are present in the system. For each weakness state what error or irregularity may occur as a result.

Allow 20 minutes for this task.

Task 3

You have been asked to prepare the audit plan for sales.

i) Complete the tables on pages 6-8 of the answer booklet to show the following tests that may be performed to achieve the objectives:

- the tests of controls;
- the tests of detail;
- the analytical procedures.

ii) State the limitations in the evidence from each of the above types of test. Use page 9 of the answer booklet.

Allow 30 minutes for this task.

Task 4

You are deciding on the sample selection for the testing of creditors.

• Using page 10 of the answer booklet:

i) state three factors you would take into account in determining your sample size;

ii) suggest, with reasons, the most appropriate population from which to select your sample when testing creditors for understatement.

Allow 15 minutes for this task.

5

Task 5

You are leading the audit of the purchases and creditors section. Your junior has prepared the working paper set out on page 11 of this booklet and has given it to you to review.

The planning notes for this work state that the objective of this purchase test is to ensure that purchases are accurately recorded, and are not overstated.

The sample size has been set at 15, and it has been decided that the sample should be selected on a systematic basis.

• Use pages 11-12 of the answer booklet to set out the review points.

Allow 25 minutes for this task.

Task 6

You are performing a creditors' statement reconciliation.

The creditors to be tested are set out on page 13 of the answer booklet. The balances that have been agreed to the statement have already been noted on the working paper. The information to complete this task is given on pages 12-14 of this booklet.

• Complete the working paper on page 13 of the answer booklet.

• Using pages 14-15 of the answer booklet, set out:

    - the objective of the test;

    - the results of your work (you should show any reconciliations);

    - any further work that is required before a conclusion can be reached.

Allow 40 minutes for this task.

Task 7

Your junior has prepared a schedule of the items included in the repairs and renewals account which he thinks may be fixed assets. It is the company's policy to capitalise amounts over £100. The schedule is on page 16 of the answer booklet.

i)   On the schedule on page 16 of the answer booklet, show which items should be treated as fixed assets by placing a tick in the column headed 'transfer to fixed assets'.

ii) On page 17 of the answer booklet, set out what additional audit tests you would perform to confirm that fixed assets are complete and accurate and that they exist.

Allow 25 minutes for this task.

Task 8

A friend of yours has a job as a waitress in the restaurant. She has seen you in the restaurant and knows that you are performing the audit. She has asked you out for a drink and has said that she wants to hear all the inside information that you have access to. She is particularly interested in what her colleagues get paid.

• Use page 18 of the answer booklet to set out how you would deal with this situation.

Allow 15 minutes for this task.

6

Task 9

The client has asked for advice on how their systems can be improved. They specifically want to ensure that they are not losing money through theft or fraud.

• Use pages 19-20 of the answer booklet to set out four weaknesses in the current system which may lead to theft or fraud, and make recommendations for improvement.

Allow 30 minutes for this task.

Task 10

The results of the sales testing seem to be inconclusive. The analytical procedures have shown that there are unexplained differences between actual and expected sales, and that the differences between the takings sheets and the tills have not been properly explained. Overall you feel that you cannot conclude on the sales work. However, although this is a material matter, it is unlikely to make the financial statements misleading.

• On pages 21-22 of the answer booklet:

i) state the type of audit report which should be given as a result of this;

ii) draft the opinion paragraph of the audit report.

Allow 20 minutes for this task.

7

DJs Ltd
Background information

DJs Ltd is a private limited company which owns a large restaurant plus a café and takeaway. The owners of the company are David Golding and John Selwood who are old friends and have run the business together for 5 years. They have 50% of the share capital each and they are both directors of the company.

David is responsible for the financial side of the business and is 'front of house' whereas John is more involved with the day-to-day running of the business. However they have recently appointed two managers who are allowing David and John to spend less time in the restaurant.

The trade is very seasonal with high turnover and profits in the summer months. However the restaurant remains open for the whole year and gains from weekenders and Christmas holiday makers. It also has an increasing local clientele.

During the summer months a large number of casual workers are taken on. Some only last a few days and are never seen again. Many are at school or college and are taking a holiday job. During the rest of the year there are around 15 people on the payroll. Most of these have been there for at least two years and that element of the workforce is fairly stable.

Many of the sales are cash sales, particularly in the café and takeaway.

Purchases are bought on credit from a number of different suppliers.

The company owns the premises from which the business is run.

8

DJs Ltd
Extracts from accounting systems notes

Monthly accounts and payroll

The company employs a bookkeeper for a few hours a month to prepare monthly accounts and the payroll. Both are prepared using Sage software. There is no password protection over the software.

The computer is kept in the office at the back of the restaurant; this is also used as a rest room for staff.

Sales

Customers can pay by cash, cheque or credit card. There is an automatic link for credit card payments so the amount is automatically transferred into the company's bank account.

A large amount of sales are paid for in cash.

At the end of each day the tills are totalled and the money in each till is counted by one of the newly appointed managers. Sales are recorded on a daily takings sheet. A comparison is made between the amount in the tills and the amount per the till rolls. However, although differences are noted, there is little or no follow up unless there is a very large difference.

On most days money from the tills is used to pay for small items. Receipts are sometimes attached to the daily sheet for these but there is no real discipline over this.

The cheques are paid into the bank on the following day. Cash is kept in a safe in the office and is used to pay for purchases and wages as much as possible. It is kept in the house which David and Peter share.

Purchases and creditors

Food orders are made by the head chef. He is also responsible for checking deliveries, to ensure that the items are in good condition and that the delivery matches the order.

David pays the invoices in the month following the date of the invoice. He matches the invoices to the statements received and clips them together. He notes the amount paid on the statement and states whether the payment was made by cash or cheque, giving the cheque number as appropriate.

The creditors at any one time are therefore usually one month's worth of purchases and expenses.

9

Payroll

Wages are paid on a fortnightly basis and are calculated from the hour sheets which the staff complete for themselves. Payments are made in cash when possible. The bookkeeper uses Sage payroll to calculate the wages but has problems in obtaining P45s, P46s, addresses, NI numbers, dates of birth etc for the staff in the summer months.

Once the bookkeeper has calculated the wages she counts out the cash and puts it in envelopes for the staff.

Fixed assets

These are purchased by David and John as required. The bookkeeper is not very reliable at posting them to the correct account and is more likely to post fixed assets to the repairs and renewals account.

10

Client	
Accounting date	

Prepared by	
Date	
Reviewed by	
Date	

Purchases

Test to ensure that purchases are correct and are not overstated.

	Purchase invoice no DJs ref	Supplier	Description	£	Included in purchases
1	22272	Nice Ice	Ice cream	185.60	✓
2	22273	Boozers	Wine	250.25	✓
3	22275	The Meat Co	Ham	132.43	✓
4	22280	The Pet Shop	Dog food	155.45	✓
5	22379	Olivers Ltd	Cooking oil	45.00	✓
6	22481	The Veg shop	Vegetables	38.70	✓
7	22511	Nice Ice	Ice cream	123.56	✓
8	22570	Foodies	Desserts	189.00	✓
9	22692	Not found	replaced by 22693		✗
	22693	Boozers	Beer	354.67	✓
10	22733	Heatons Ltd	Ingredients	65.54	✓
11	22815	The News	Christmas advert	87.50	✓
12	22896	Coffee Club	Coffee	67.89	✓

Conclusion

Purchases are correctly recorded.

Supplier statement to non ledger

Suppliers' statements

OLIVER'S LTD
Cooking oil for the catering trade
2 The Industrial Estate, Highestoft, Suffolk

Customer name: DJs Ltd
Address: 2 The Sea Front, Suffolk

	debit £	credit £	balance £
Brought forward			540.59
14/10/02 inv. 30741	100.00		640.50
21/10/02 inv. 30814	176.60		817.10
28/10/02 inv. 30902	108.10		925.20
31/10/02 payment – thank you		817.10	108.10
06/11/02 inv. 31102	180.60		288.70
13/11/02 inv. 31198	131.80		420.50
20/11/02 inv. 31281	308.60		729.10
28/11/02 inv. 31350	141.70		870.80
30/11/02 payment – thank you		420.50	450.30
02/12/02 inv. 31423	109.00		559.30
12/12/02 inv. 31534	218.00		777.30
20/12/02 inv. 31678	196.20		973.50
Balance due at 31/12/02			973.50

THE VEG SHOP
1 HIGH STREET
SUFFOLK

03/01/03

THE FOLLOWING INVOICES ARE OUTSTANDING:
No 1127   15/12/02   £120.70
No 1842   22/12/01   £99.64
Total   £220.34

Please pay immediately

12

145

Suppliers' statements (continued)

BOOZERS 17 WINES WAY INDUSTRIAL ESTATE SUFFOLK			STATEMENT 31 DECEMBER 2002	

Date	Transaction		Amount £	Balance £
30/11/02	Balance forward			5,202.67
06/12/02	Invoice DJ125		75.65	5,278.32
12/12/02	Invoice DJ187		608.40	5,886.72
27/12/02	Invoice DJ254		84.70	5,971.42

Current	1-30 days	31-60 days	61-90 days	Over 90 days	Amount due
768.75	3,385.51	1,817.16	-	-	5,971.42

[Handwritten annotations:]

Very Short c/Note

210.10
10 24
220 34

Clint Bal   4065.56
Payment in trans   1817.16
Inv in trans   84 70
Bal per Stalent   5971 42

Olives   Clint Bal   1036.90
Payments outstanding   817 10
2 9 40
1036 50
Input error   63 00
973 50

13

Creditors ledgers

Boozers

Tp	Date	Ref	Details	Balance
Balance				5,202.67
PI	06/12/02	22873	DJ125	75.65
PI	12/12/02	22901	DJ187	608.40
PA	30/12/02			-1,817.16
			Total	4,069.56

check '8470. missing.

Olivers Ltd

Tp	Date	Ref	Details	Balance
PI	28/10/02	22604	30902	108.10
PI	06/11/02	22636	31102	180.60
PI	13/11/02	22741	31198	131.80
PI	20/11/02	22793	31281	308.60
PI	28/11/02	22801	31350	141.70
PA	28/11/02		payment	-420.50
PI	02/12/02	22852	31423	109.00
PI	12/12/02	22871	31534	281.00
PI	20/12/02	22915	31678	196.20
			Total	1,036.50

218.00

payment 817.10.

The Veg Shop

Tp	Date	Ref	Details	Balance
PI	08/12/02	22864	1011	140.20
PC	08/12/02	c103	credit note	-10.24
PA	10/12/02	22858	payment	-140.20
PI	15/12/02	22901	1127	120.70
PI	22/12/02	22928	1842	99.64
			Total	210.10

C/Note

Boozers Client Bal 4069.56.

Bal on Statement 5971.42.

14

REVISED STANDARDS
TECHNICIAN STAGE
NVQ/SVQ IN ACCOUNTING LEVEL 4
SPECIMEN SIMULATION

AAT

**ASSOCIATION
OF ACCOUNTING
TECHNICIANS**

SIMULATION—SPECIMEN

IMPLEMENTING AUDITING PROCEDURES

ANSWER BOOKLET

TO BE COMPLETED BY CANDIDATE

Candidate Name

Registration Number

AAC Code

This is my own unaided work

Signed

Date

TO BE COMPLETED BY ASSESSOR

Assessor Name

Date

Overall simulation result: Satisfactory?:   Y / N

Comments

Note to assessor:
This booklet must remain sealed until the time of the assessment.

Note to candidate:
This booklet must be returned to your assessor.

© AAT 2003
154 Clerkenwell Road, London EC1R 5AD   Tel: +44 (0)20 7837 8600   Fax: +44 (0)20 7837 6970

ANSWERS (Task 1)

Client	DJ		Prepared by	
Accounting date	31/12/02		Date	
			Reviewed by	
			Date	

I think the following have been
selected for particular attention
because

Sales: The business does
not a lot of cash sales so
there is a risk that sales
could be under mis-stated
or there is scope for theft.

Purchases & Creditors

~~There could be~~
There is a risk that the
+ Creditors would be mis-stated
~~as some are paid for in cash~~
~~as by ones~~ as there are a
large number of transactions in
a month so there is scope
for errors. ~~As creditors is a material~~ ~~leads to be~~
is likely to be one of the
most material areas of the audit

2

ANSWERS (Task 1, continued)

Client	
Accounting date	

Prepared by	
Date	
Reviewed by	
Date	

Creditors figure is going to be one of the most significant figure on the bal sheet.

Payroll

As the are a lot of temp staff over the summer this could lead to errors in calc PAYE

Fixed Assets.

Errors could result in assets being treated as r + r. so this could lead to misstatement of Assets in the Bal sheet and Misstatement in P&L A/c

3

ANSWERS (Task 2)

Client		Prepared by	
Accounting date		Date	
		Reviewed by	
		Date	

Weakness	Error or irregularity
No password protectn	As this office is also used by all staff, anyone can assess the system
Invoices not matched to Del/notes orders.	As present del nots matched to orders but no invoices. This could lead to paying for goods not ordred/received

4

ANSWERS (Task 2, continued)

Client	
Accounting date	

Prepared by	
Date	
Reviewed by	
Date	

Weakness	Error or irregularity
Receipts are not always attached to daily sheets for money put out for exp.	If staff know it doesn't matter if no receipt is received this could lead to staff taking money for themselves.
No follow up on different illusts to follow	Could lead to newly appointed managers or staff taking small amounts for themselves which could add to to a large amount over time

5

ANSWERS (Task 3)

Client		Prepared by	
Accounting date		Date	
		Reviewed by	
		Date	

Audit objectives:
All sales are recorded.
Sales have been recorded accurately.

Tests of control

Observe sales are entered into the till at time of sale

Check sales records sheets to till rolls.
Check sales records sheets totals are entered correctly in a/c system
Check sales records sheets to bank statements.

Review comparisons of sales record Sheets to till roll that this is being done even though it is only on large amounts

6

ANSWERS (Task 3, continued)

Client	
Accounting date	

Prepared by	
Date	
Reviewed by	
Date	

Audit objectives:
All sales are recorded.
Sales have been recorded accurately.

Tests of details

Check sales record sheets to till roll

Check " " " to bank statement

Check " " " totals are entered
in a/c correctly

7

155

ANSWERS (Task 3, continued)

Client		Prepared by	
Accounting date		Date	
		Reviewed by	
		Date	

Audit objectives:
All sales are recorded.
Sales have been recorded accurately.

Analytical procedures

~~Check~~ Compare sales figures by
mark to ~~test year sales~~ preceding years

Check ~~orders~~ of ~~sales~~
ex

Compare sales to purchases
via gross profit %

Compare sales to expenses to
make sure the appropriate
proportion

8

ANSWERS (Task 3, continued)

Client		Prepared by	
Accounting date		Date	
		Reviewed by	
		Date	

Limitations of audit evidence

Tests of control

Observing – This may not be helpful
& people behave differently when
they are being observed.

Tests of details

Test can only be done on sales actually
recorded. If a sales has been made
but N been entered the test will not
pick it up.

Analytical procedures

In a business like this it is very
difficult to make accurate predictions
Company sales to purchases can be
a give good evidence only
If he is sure that sales are
current or visa vesta and not
company sale by any other means.

9

ANSWERS (Task 4)

Client		Prepared by	
Accounting date		Date	
		Reviewed by	
		Date	

~~I would select~~

It would depend on the number of creditors used

The materiality of the balance

10

ANSWERS (Task 5)

Client	
Accounting date	

Prepared by	
Date	
Reviewed by	
Date	

_____

_____

_____

_____

_____

_____

_____

_____

_____

_____

_____

_____

_____

_____

_____

_____

_____

_____

_____

_____

_____

_____

11

ANSWERS (Task 5, continued)

Client	
Accounting date	

Prepared by	
Date	
Reviewed by	
Date	

12

ANSWERS (Task 6)

Client	
Accounting date	

Prepared by	
Date	
Reviewed by	
Date	

Creditors statement reconciliation

Creditor	Balance per client (£)	Balance per statement (£)	Agrees to statement	Reconciled
Boozers	4,069.56	5,971.42	✓	
Jo Bakers	425.35	425.35	✓	
Coffee Club	1,287.10	Not available		
Foodies	3,924.50	3,924.50	✓	
Heatons	1,008.18	Not available		
The Meat Club	2,478.64	2,478.64	✓	
Olivers Ltd	1,036.50	973.50	✓	
The Veg Shop	210.10	220.34	✓	

13

ANSWERS (Task 6, continued)

Client			Prepared by	
Accounting date			Date	
			Reviewed by	
			Date	

Objective of test.

To confirm balances are correct.
(Comparing with ledger with
external memos (supplier statement)).

2 creditors not replied.
to chase up.

ANSWERS (Task 6, continued)

Client	
Accounting date	

Prepared by	
Date	
Reviewed by	
Date	

15

ANSWERS (Task 7)

Client	
Accounting date	

Prepared by	
Date	
Reviewed by	
Date	

Fixed assets: review of repairs and renewals

	£	Transfer to fixed assets
Replacement Plates	1,670	✓
Maintenance of tills	400	
Computer software	150	
New chairs for outside	2,500	✓
Paper napkins	357	
Repair of fridge	125	
Coffee making machine	4,500	✓
Decorator: wall papering restaurant	500	
Annual maintenance of security system	200	
Grass cutting: weekly	500	
Repair of dishwasher	97	
Replacement dishwasher	980	✓
Picture hanging	125	
Mural painted on restaurant wall	900	
Plant care	3,000	
New cutlery	5,000	✓
Tea towels	200	
Sign writing for outside	350	

16

ANSWERS (Task 7, continued)

Client		Prepared by	
Accounting date		Date	
		Reviewed by	
		Date	

Completeness   Account   Existing

Check Invoices of Purchase
Invoice to co.
Check value on invoice to
list,
Physical check that items
exist.

17

ANSWERS (Task 8)

Client			Prepared by	
Accounting date			Date	
			Reviewed by	
			Date	

All clnt info is confidental.

18

ANSWERS (Task 9)

Client			Prepared by	
Accounting date			Date	
			Reviewed by	
			Date	

Objective: to ensure money is not lost through theft or fraud.

Current situation	Recommendation for improvement
Use passwords No	Protect info with passwords
Also cash pd out for exp fm till	No cash given out unless a receipt given.

19

ANSWERS (Task 9, continued)

Client	
Accounting date	

Prepared by	
Date	
Reviewed by	
Date	

Objective: to ensure money is not lost through theft or fraud.

Current situation	Recommendation for improvement
P/Ordrs authord by dreckrs + return to plorder del nut / Invoice.	
	true sheets to bee authorisd by manger

20

ANSWERS (Task 10)

Client	
Accounting date	

Prepared by	
Date	
Reviewed by	
Date	

_____

_____

_____

_____

_____

_____

_____

_____

_____

_____

_____

_____

_____

_____

_____

_____

_____

_____

_____

_____

_____

_____

21

ANSWERS (Task 10, continued)

Client	
Accounting date	

Prepared by	
Date	
Reviewed by	
Date	

22

ANSWERS

answers to chapter 1:
THE BUSINESS ENVIRONMENT

1   A registered company must keep the following records:

- Records of money spent and received by the company from day to day
- Details of what the money related to (sales, purchases and wages)
- Details of the assets and liabilities of the company
- Statements of stock held at the financial yearend
- Records of the stock count from which the above statements were made
- Invoices of goods sold and purchased

2   An audit is an examination by an independent qualified examiner to ensure that the financial statement of a company, prepared from the accounting records by the directors, give a true and fair view of the company's affairs and transactions in the year.

Most companies are required by law to have an audit. However, there are exemptions for small companies (private companies with a turnover of less than £5.6 million and a balance sheet total of less than £2.8 million), charitable companies (charities with a gross income of less than £500,000 and a balance sheet total of less than £2.8 million) and dormant companies (companies for whom it has been unnecessary to record a transaction in the financial year).

answers to chapter 2: INTRODUCTION TO AUDIT

1   External audit

External audit is an exercise carried out by qualified persons, independent of the company, to determine whether the financial statements of that company, prepared by the directors of that company, give a true and fair view of the state of the company's affairs at the period end and the profit or loss of the company for that period.

Most companies are required by law to have an external audit, hence it is often referred to as a statutory audit. Some companies, if they are small or dormant, may be exempt from the requirement to have an audit by law, however, they may still choose to have such an independent audit.

Internal audit

Internal audit is a function of the business that can be set up by management to carry out such duties as monitoring internal controls and carrying out special audits for the directors as they require them.

Differences

The key differences are highlighted by the descriptions above. External auditors are independent of the business and report to the owners, internal auditors are by contrast employees of the business and report to the managers. External auditors focus on the financial statements of the company, internal auditors look more at the systems of the business, and the business as a whole.

External audits are required by law, whereas there is no such requirement for companies to have an internal audit department, and in fact, only larger companies tend to have them, so internal audits are more rare than external audits.

2   The advantages of having an audit include the following:

(a)   Shareholders who are not involved in management gain reassurance from audited accounts about management's stewardship of the business.

(b)   Audited accounts are a reliable source for a fair valuation of shares in an unquoted company either for taxation or other purposes.

(c)   Some banks rely on accounts for the purposes of making loans and reviewing the value of security.

(d) Creditors and potential creditors can use audited accounts to assess the potential strength of the company.

(e) The audit provides management with an useful independent check on the accuracy of the accounting systems; the auditors can recommend improvements in those systems.

3 Auditors have a contract with the company (which in English law is all the shareholders acting as a body). English law implies a term into that contract which states that the auditors have a duty of care to the company.

If the auditors breach this duty of care, the company may be able to sue the auditors for negligence, if the breach of the duty caused financial loss to the company.

In contrast, even if third parties believe that the auditors have been negligent in their audit and this has caused them loss, they may not be able to make a similar claim for negligence.

This is because a duty of care existing is a key aspect of the legal concept of negligence, and the courts have previously determined that auditors do not automatically have a duty of care to third parties.

If third parties want to sue auditors for negligence, they have to prove that a duty of care exists between the audit firm and themselves, which is not presumed under the law, although particular facts may have created such a duty – for example, if the auditor has agreed with the third party that he does have such a duty.

4 **Auditing Practices Board**

The Auditing Practices Board (APB) is an independent body that issues professional guidance for auditors to follow. It is a constituent body of the Financial Reporting Council (FRC), which is the independent regulator of accounting and auditing in the UK. The Government has delegated responsibility for standard setting and monitoring to the FRC.

Auditors in the UK are required to follow the professional standards issued by the APB. These standards are standards on how to audit, known as International Standards on Auditing (UK and Ireland) and ethical standards, which outline how auditors should behave and, in particular, how they should remain independent of their clients.

5 An audit report specifically states that it is planned and performed to obtain information and explanations which the auditor considers necessary to provide reasonable assurance that the accounts are free from material misstatement, whether caused by irregularity or error.

As such the auditor does not examine each and every transaction in detail to ensure that it is correctly recorded and properly presented. The audit report is not a certificate of accuracy but an expression of the auditor's opinion as to whether the accounts reflect a true and fair view of its financial position on a specific date and its results for a specific period.

The view given in accounts is based on a combination of both fact and judgement and therefore cannot be characterised as either 'absolute' or 'correct'.

6 **Working papers**

Working papers are the documents on which auditors record their audit work. They may be paper format or on a computer.

Working papers must contain certain details. For example, they must state the name of the client, the year end being worked on, the name of the auditor doing the work and the date the work was done. They should also state the audit area, and contain the work done.

Audit files

Working papers are kept in audit files. There are two types of audit file; a current audit file, in which all the papers relevant to one year's audit are kept, and a permanent audit file, in which working papers of ongoing relevance to future audits are kept. For example, the engagement letter (see below) is kept in the permanent audit file.

Engagement letter

The audit engagement letter is the letter which sets out the terms of agreement between the audit firm and the client in respect of the audit. It must be signed by the client, to ensure that he understands the terms of the agreement between the parties, before the first audit is undertaken.

After that it will cover subsequent audits until the agreement is terminated.

It might be necessary to reissue an engagement letter in certain circumstances, for example, if there is a change in the terms of agreement between the parties, or if there is a substantial change in a key factor – for example, the company reorganises itself or purchases a subsidiary company.

At the moment, some audit firms are amending their letters of engagement to take advantage of the provisions of Companies Act 2006 setting a limit on the liability of the auditor.

7   **Confidentiality**

The auditor has a duty to keep company affairs private. The auditor is likely to come across sensitive information when carrying out his audit and must not use that information to the advantage of a third party or to his own advantage.

In respect of the information concerning the director's intentions to sell the business, this information will impact on certain aspects of the audit work to be undertaken. However, the auditors have a duty not to mention this to other members of staff at Glad Rags and to be circumspect with the information when attending the client – for example, not leaving working papers making reference to it lying around and even being discreet if wanting to talk to the director about it.

8   In the current business environment there is likely to be a lot of competitive pressure to provide clients with a service which matches their specific needs. This may entail developing a good understanding of the client's business and often auditors may feel they need to 'get close to the client' to be able to build a good working relationship and hence deliver an effective service.

However, the auditor's primary role is to provide an independent audit opinion on the client's accounts. There are a variety of factors that may adversely impact on an auditor's independence. Two of the factors which are relevant in this case are:

–   The development of close personal relationships between client personnel and audit personnel

–   Acceptance of expensive goods and hospitality from the client.

Being able to jump a three-year waiting list for a football season ticket is likely to be viewed as a big favour which could compromise your independence. Even if you are not of the mind to give in to client pressure, the client may feel in a position to exert pressure.

Sharing an executive box with the directors on a regular basis may entail receiving a certain amount of hospitality. It may also give the wrong impression to the world in general.

9   Auditors have a duty of confidentiality to their clients and are required to keep information obtained in the course of their audit private, perhaps even from members of staff of the client.

Auditors therefore have to take care over the security of their audit files, which might contain sensitive information, such as payroll information, or other information that the directors do not want other staff to know.

Given that the client has provided a key to the office, Clare's best option if she wanted to leave the room would have been to lock the room and leave a note of where she had gone. Alternatively, if the team has taken lockable audit cases to the audit, she might have locked the files away before leaving the room unlocked.

10   The auditors will have to consider whether this represents a risk for the audit. However, Peter is experienced in the business and is likely to be able to draw on the assistance of his father if required, so in terms of carrying out the audit, it is unlikely that this raises the risk of the audit substantially.

However, the auditors will have to consider whether this change in senior management necessitates the audit firm re-issuing the letter of engagement between the audit firm and the company, to ensure that the managing director is fully aware of the terms of the audit.

Given that Peter Green has not previously been involved with the audit, it is probably wise to reissue the audit engagement letter, even though the terms of the audit engagement have not changed. This will ensure that the only working director of the company fully understands the relationship between the company and the audit firm.

11   Auditors' liability depends on whether negligent accountants owed a duty of care to those who have relied on their accounts. If the auditors knew a third party would rely and they failed to disclaim liability, they could be found liable.

(a)   **The possibility of demonstrating negligence**

All APB pronouncements and in particular Auditing Standards are likely to be taken into account when the adequacy of the work of auditors is being considered in a court of law or in other contested situations.

In the case of Leesmoor Ltd, the auditors did not attend to observe the company's physical stocktaking (inventory count) procedures as recommended by ISA 501 Audit evidence – Additional considerations for specific items. Whether this was negligent would depend on whether or not the auditors could satisfy the court as to whether there were good practical reasons for non?attendance and the other audit work which they carried out in relation to stock provided sufficient appropriate audit evidence on which to base their opinion. This may prove to be difficult as the ISA suggests that attendance at the stocktake is normally the best way of proving existence.

(b) **The fact that the stocks figure in the financial statements apparently 'made sense'**

This suggests that the main audit evidence on which the auditors based their opinion, in relation to the stocks figure, was the result of their analytical procedures in this area. As the auditors seem, through pressure of work, to have neglected to attend the stocktake, then one would expect them to have carried out more extensive analytical procedures than would perhaps normally have been the case for that client. If it appeared that the auditors had only carried out a minimal amount of procedures, then they would very likely be open to a charge of negligence.

(c) **The fact that the auditors were not informed that the financial statements were to be used to obtain additional finance**

Past case law shows that judges do not care to attribute a duty of care to unknown third parties. Following the law in Caparo, it is unlikely that a judge would rule that the auditors had a duty of care to the lenders.

answers to chapter 3:
THE COMPANY ENVIRONMENT (CONTROLS)

1   The five components of an internal control system are:

-   Control environment
-   The entity's risk assessment process
-   Information system
-   Control activities
-   Monitoring of controls

2   The control environment is the attitudes, awareness and actions of management and those charged with governance about internal control and its importance.

As directors are those people charged with governance in a company, and in many companies, particularly smaller companies are also those who manage a company on a day-to-day basis, they directly impact the control environment.

This can be a positive impact or a negative impact. If directors themselves override controls set up in a company and give other staff the impression that controls are not important, then they will be strongly contributing to a poor control environment.

On the other hand, if the directors follow control activities themselves and encourage others to do so, if they promote an attitude in a company that internal control is important, and encourage staff to monitor their own performance and the performance of others in observing control, then they can contribute to an excellent control environment.

3   An information system is an infrastructure which carries information for a company and compiles a body of information from individual pieces of information. For example, a sales invoice is entered into the information system and is converted into information about overall sales for the month or the year.

A system that is manual is an information system that is heavily documented in paper format, for example in physical ledgers. A system that is computerised is one which is retained predominantly in electronic format – so information is input to a computer and processed through that.

In practice, most information systems in companies are a combination of manual and computerised but will tend to being one or the other. In modern times, particularly in large companies, the trend is that systems are increasingly computerised.

4 Control activities

Control activities are the policies and procedures that help ensure that management directives about internal control are carried out. They are often simply referred to as 'controls'.

There are various types of control activities. The following are examples:

Approval – for example, a company will not place an order for goods until a senior member of staff has approved that order.

General computer controls – for example, company staff will be issued with passwords to access computers so that the computers cannot be accessed by external persons.

Application controls – for example, programmed controls in a computer to highlight entries that are not logical (for example, if the VAT figure on a sales invoice is not 17.5% of the sales total).

Arithmetical controls – for example, staff ensuring that invoices add up correctly.

Maintaining control accounts/trial balances

Performing reconciliations – for example, reconciling the bank balance per the cashbook to the bank balance per the bank statement to ensure that errors have not been made.

Comparing assets to records – for example, doing a physical fixed asset count and comparing existing assets to those recorded in a fixed asset register.

Restricting access – for example, locking the storeroom so that raw materials cannot be misappropriated.

5 Extending credit to customers

The risks associated with extending credit to customers are:

- Customers will not pay for the goods and the company will lose the value of them

- Customers do not pay promptly for goods, meaning that the company loses out on the value of interest it could otherwise be earning on that money

Control activities

The company can mitigate the above risks by implementing certain controls. For example, they can ensure that they do not accept new customers until they have carried out credit checks on them to ensure that they are capable of paying their bills. In addition, they can allocate existing and new customers with credit limits, to ensure that they limit the amount of their exposure to not being paid. Lastly, they can not accept orders from customers who have outstanding invoices over the credit terms that they have been offered.

6 Despatching goods and invoicing

Risks associated with despatching goods and invoicing:

- The company can send out goods and not invoice them, therefore losing their value
- The company can invoice wrongly and lose money
- The company can overcharge and lose customers

Control activities

The company can mitigate these risks by recording all dispatches and matching invoices with those records to ensure that invoices are correct. They can check invoices before they are sent out to ensure that they are calculated correctly do not contain costly errors.

7   **Controls present**

- Necessity for orders is evidenced prior to ordering and a requisition is raised

- The company has a policy for choosing suppliers

- Goods received are examined for quantity and quality

- Goods received are checked against the order

- Supplier invoices are checked to the order

- Supplier invoices are checked for prices, quantities and calculations and given a reference number

- Purchases are entered on the purchase ledger promptly

- Cheque requests are presented for approval with supporting documentation

- Supplier statements are reconciled to the purchase ledger

- The purchase ledger control account is regularly reconciled with the purchase ledger list of balances

8   **Controls – machinists**

- Pieces worked are recorded
- Pieces worked are reviewed
- Payroll is prepared by the director prior to payment
- Identity of staff is verified prior to payment

Controls – other staff

Payroll is prepared by the director prior to payment

9   **Controls in the sales system**

- Tills have passwords for each cashier
- Tills are locked when not in use
- Sales are recorded on the tills rolls and analysed by type of sale
- Till receipts are reconciled with cash and credit slips daily
- Sales are recorded in ledgers daily
- Cash is kept securely in the tills and banked daily

10 Brief to audit junior

(a) Batch control totals ensure that data processed through a computerised accounting system is processed completely and accurately.

Examples of control totals include the following:

(i) Record counts: the total number of purchase invoices processed.

(ii) Value totals: the total value of purchase invoices processed.

(iii) Hash totals: this is a total which has no accounting significance other than as a check on completeness of processing, for example adding up the supplier purchase ledger account numbers.

(b) Programmed controls should include the following:

(i) Field checks: these should ensure that all relevant data is entered before a transaction can proceed.

(ii) Check digits: these are used to ensure the correctness of data, the reasonableness of which cannot otherwise be checked, for example supplier account numbers.

(iii) Range limits: these should ensure that the data entered is reasonable, for example all purchase invoices over a certain amount should be rejected.

(iv) Matching of input to a standing data file: this should ensure the reasonableness of items input, for example a supplier only supplying appropriate goods.

(v) Exception reports: these should highlight items requiring further review, for example invoices or balances with suppliers over a certain amount.

(vi) Sequence checks: these should check that all purchase invoices within a certain sequence have been processed, and highlight any numbers that have not been.

(vii) Existence checks: these should ensure items entered correspond to valid standing data, for example a supplier number is the number of an account that is actually on the purchase ledger (payables ledger).

(viii) Batch totals: the value of all items input should be calculated and compared with the total calculated before the items were input.

(ix) Reminders: the computer should not allow exit from the processing function without asking whether input is to be saved.

(x) Resubmission of rejected inputs: a report should be printed detailing all items that the computer has rejected. This report should be reviewed by management.

Note: only five controls were asked for.

(c) (i) New purchase ledger accounts should be authorised by a senior manager before being entered onto the purchase ledger.

Auditors should review a sample of input forms for new suppliers, and check that they have been appropriately authorised.

(ii)   All changes to standing data should be authorised by a senior manager before being input. Managers should also compare output reports with input forms to confirm that changes have been made correctly.

Auditors should check input forms and output reports for evidence of management authorisation and review, and compare the documentation to see if the review has been carried out thoroughly.

(iii)   Supplier accounts that have been inactive for a significant time should be reviewed, and management should authorise deletion if the accounts are dormant.

Auditors should check for evidence of review, and check deletions have been authorised by management. Auditors should enquire why any accounts with other than nil balances on have been deleted.

(iv)   Standing data should be printed out regularly and compared to other evidence of supplier details, for example phone book entries or supplier invoices.

Auditors should check a sample of printouts for evidence of management review, and reperform the review.

(v)   Access to standing data should be limited by a system of passwords.

Auditors should attempt to access standing data using an invalid password, and make enquiries about the password system to assess the strength (are passwords changed regularly, not shown on the screen, are terminals shut down after a certain time if not used?).

answers to chapter 4:
AUDITING SYSTEMS

1   Auditors may record systems by using:

- Narrative notes
- Flowcharts
- Internal control questionnaires

2   A walkthrough test is a test designed to ensure that the system operates as the auditors have been told that it does. They select a transaction in a particular area (for example, a sale or a purchase) and trace it through the company's information system from the initial point (for example, the sale order, or the purchase requisition).

3   The auditor may take a combined approach, where he will test controls and then reduce his subsequent substantive testing (although he must always carry out tests of detail on material items), or a substantive approach, where he does not test controls, but instead renders control risk as high and conducts more tests of detail instead.

4   If auditors decide to test controls, then they are required to ensure that controls have operated effectively throughout the year. They will therefore often carry out tests of control at interim audits during the course of the financial year rather than leaving all the controls testing until the final audit, which takes place after the yearend.

	Question	Yes/No	Comment
5	Are orders only accepted from low credit risks?	Yes	Sales staff check that customers have not exceeded limits.
	Are despatches checked by appropriate personnel?	Yes	Ian Jones checks order prior to despatch.
	Are goods sent out recorded?	Yes	Ian Jones raises a despatch note.
	Are customers required to give evidence of receipt of goods?	Yes	They are requested to sign a copy of the despatch note.
	Are invoices checked to despatch notes and invoices?	Yes	The order and despatch note are matched prior to invoicing.
	Are invoices prepared using authorised prices?	Yes	The sales department have completed authorised prices on the order. Jane does not appear to carry out additional checks on invoices.
	Are invoices checked to ensure they add up correctly?	No	Jane does not appear to carry out additional checks on invoices.
	Are sales receipts matched with invoices?	No	No. Receipts are simply posted to the ledger and cashbook.
	Are statements sent out regularly?	Yes	Monthly
	Are overdue accounts reviewed regularly?	No	No review appears to take place, but bad debts are rare.
	Are there safeguards over post received to ensure that cheques are not intercepted?	No	Post is opened elsewhere and transferred to the accounts department.
	Are bankings made daily?	No	However, cheques are kept securely until they are banked.
	Would it be appropriate to perform tests of control in this area? (Give reason/reasons in the comments box.)	Yes	There appears to be a good system of control over ordering, despatch, invoicing and recording. Substantive tests should also be carried out over receipts and bad debts where controls are weakest.

6   Weakness: invoicing

When invoices are raised, they are not checked to ensure that the additions are correct.

Consequence

Invoices could contain errors of calculation resulting in loss to the company.

Recommendation

Invoices should be checked prior to being sent out to customers to ensure that they add correctly and that VAT has been calculated correctly. Ideally this check should be done by someone other than Jane, for example Beth, as it might be easier for someone unfamiliar with the invoices to identify errors.

Weakness: receipts

Post opening appears to be unsupervised and no initial list of receipts is made. Customer remittances do not appear to be retained.

Implication

Receipts could be lost or misappropriated on arrival at the company.

Recommendation

Ideally, someone from the accounts department should attend the opening of the post and make an initial list of receipts. Customer remittances should be retained so that receipts can be reconciled to specific invoices.

Other potential weaknesses:

1) Ideally banking should be done daily, but if there are insufficient receipts to justify this, the system in place to keep cheques secure until banking is sufficient.

2) Ideally, sales ledger accounts should be reviewed regularly to ensure amounts are not overdue. However, bad debts are rare, so this is not essential.

7 Tests of controls

Controls (as identified in answers to Chapter 3 questions)	Tests of control
Necessity for orders is evidenced prior to ordering and a requisition is raised	Review a sample of requisitions. Enquire about re-order levels with stores manager.
The company has a policy for choosing suppliers	Review a sample of orders to ensure that the suppliers appear on the approved list.
Goods received are examined for quantity and quality	Observe the stores manager receiving some goods.
Goods received are checked against the order	Observe the stores manager receiving some goods. Scrutinise a sample of orders for evidence of the check.
Supplier invoices are checked to the order	Observe the accounts assistant checking supplier invoices.
Supplier invoices are checked for prices, quantities and calculations and given a reference number	Scrutinise a sample of supplier invoices for evidence of the checks.
Purchases are entered on the purchase ledger promptly	Observe the accounts assistant doing the invoice routine.
Cheque requests are presented for approval with supporting documentation	Scrutinise paid invoices for any evidence of approval. Observe the cheque payments routine.
Supplier statements are reconciled to the purchase ledger	Scrutinise a sample of reconciliations.
The purchase ledger control account is regularly reconciled with the purchase ledger list of balances	Scrutinise a sample of reconciliations.

8 Tests of controls

Controls (as identified in answers to Chapter 3 questions)	Tests of control
Pieces worked are recorded	Review records of pieces worked.
Pieces worked are reviewed	Scrutinise the exception report and look for evidence of authorisation.
Payroll is prepared by director	Review payroll and check that it is indeed prepared by the director.
Identify of staff is verified prior to cash payments being made	Attend a wages payout and observe the controls in operation.

9   **Weakness: counting of cash**

Presently, cash is counted by the cashiers who have taken the cash in the first place.

Implication

This is a weakness, as it would be possible to perpetrate a fraud by recording smaller takings on the till rolls than have actually been paid and removing the overpayment of cash when the cash was counted.

Recommendation

Cash should be counted by different staff members, or cashiers should count the cash in a different till from the one they have manned. Cash counts should always be supervised.

Weakness: counting of cash

Cash counts do not always start on time and therefore there is a risk that cash is still being counted when the shop is opened to the public.

Implication

Exposure of the unlocked tills to the public is dangerous as it increases the risk of theft by a customer and puts the cashiers counting the cash at personal risk.

Recommendation

Cash counts must start on time, or be moved to the evening so that this risk does not arise. If cash were counted in the evening, it could still be kept in the locked safes until the next day for banking so that it was secure, alternatively it could be kept together in one company safe which fewer people knew the combination for (see next weakness).

Weakness: passwords and general security

The individual passwords used to protect the tills are widely known and used by more than one individual.

Implication

A greater number of people have access to the cash than is strictly necessary, meaning that it is more at risk of misappropriation. The poor controls over general security mean that it would be easier for a person to carry out frauds on cash (such as discussed above) and cover their own tracks so that they could not personally be held responsible.

Recommendation

Passwords should be renewed frequently and management must press the importance of this control and encourage staff to keep them secret. They might have to consider imposing punishment for shared passwords.

10   Task 1

Potential misstatements	Controls identified	Control objective satisfied
An employee could order goods for own personal use and charge them to the company.	Orders are approved by Mrs Clementine.	Valid.
Incorrect quantities received.	When goods arrive quantities are checked against the PO, and a 3-part GRN raised.	Recorded, valid, timely, classified.
Goods received but no GRN raised.	Cyclical stock counts.	Recorded, valid, timely.
Not all goods received are recorded in stock.	Cyclical stock counts. GRN procedures.	Recorded, valid, timely.
GRNs may be raised but not received by accounts payable.	Review of unmatched purchase orders.	Recorded, timely.
Invoices might not be received.	Review of unmatched GRNs.	Recorded, valid, timely.
Invoices might be incorrect.	Invoice calculation checked, details agreed to PO/GRN, prices agreed to supplier's standard price list. Matched to GRN.	Valued, recorded, valid, timely.
Batched invoices may not be input to the purchase ledger – individually omitted or batch not processed.	Supplier statement reconciliations. Input/output check for invoices processed. Batch book review.	Recorded, valid, valued, timely, classified, posted.
Pay an incorrect amount.	Invoices are coded and authorised for payment.	Valid, valued, classified.
Invoices may be input, but incorrectly.	Input/output check for invoices processed.	Recorded, valued, classified.

Potential misstatements	Controls identified	Control objective satisfied
Purchase ledger may not be updated, or may be updated incorrectly.	Purchase ledger is automatically updated by the computer. Purchase ledger control account reconciliations. Supplier statement reconciliations.	Recorded, valid, valued, timely, classified, posted.
Nominal ledger may not be updated, or may be updated incorrectly.	Purchase ledger control account reconciliation.	Posted.
Debit notes may be raised which are invalid, or raised twice.	Credit notes matched to debit notes. Review of unmatched debit notes.	Recorded, valid.
Credit notes could be batched and input twice to the purchase ledger.	Purchase ledger is automatically updated by the computer. Purchase ledger recs, supplier statement recs.	Recorded, valid, valued, timely, classified, posted.
Credit notes may be input, but incorrectly.	Input/output check for documents processed.	Recorded, valued, classified.

Task 2

We should decide to rely on the system because there are appropriate controls, including supplier statement reconciliations, which would detect failure arising from weaknesses identified.

11 **Objective** To obtain evidence that invoices are matched to Goods Received Notes and are properly authorised.

Work done Selected a sample of 10 invoices from the PLL and:

(a) Ensured the invoice had been initialled as evidence of matching to GRN and authorisation.

(b) Reperformed matching of invoice to GRN.

Results See next page.

There have been two control failures in the sample selected:

(a) One invoice was not authorised.
(b) One invoice was authorised but the GRN did not match the invoice.

Conclusion The controls tested do not appear to be operating effectively. We must either extend our sample size and/or amend our decision to rely on this control and/or consider whether an alternative control is available.

Invoice number	Date	Supplier	Goods (per invoice)		GRN No	
100948	31/01/X3	Green Forest Timber	500m 6cm planking	A	19474	✓
101896	26/02/X3	Pots of Paint	300 ltrs Eggshell white 300 ltrs Eggshell black 50 ltrs Vinyl silk pink	A	19593	✓
102844	20/03/X3	Bluegrass Farm	20 pints milk 1 sack potatoes 1 sack carrots 3 doz eggs	A	19738	✓
103792	18/04/X3	Blix Hardware	20,000 1" nails 10,000 2" nails 5,000 brackets	(1)	19888	✓
104740	16/05/X3	Henhao Timber	4,000m 6cm Grade A Beechwood	A	19975	✓
105688	14/06/X3	Ardwick Accessories	400 Brass door knobs 800 Brass hinges 400 Brass keyholes 400 Brass lock mechanisms	A	20059	✓
106636	10/07/X3	Touch of Glass Ltd	400 Security panels 400 Glass cutters	A	20196 20310	✓
107584	11/08/X3	Mustafa	40m 3cm oak planks 30m 4cm oak planks	A	20430	(2)
108532	05/09/X3	Paper March	60 reams A4 letterhead	A	20556	✓

Audit ticks

A = Invoice authorised   (1) No authorisation

✓ = Agreed details to GRN   (2) Details do not agreed to GRN

12 **Tutorial note:** the letter would include any other weaknesses and conclude with the standard paragraphs inviting responses and action which you were not expected to produce. Note that the question only asked you for weaknesses in the computerised system.

PQR Associates
Certified Accountants
151 Any St
Edinburgh ED6 8DJ

31 March 20X2

Members of the Board,

Financial statements for the year ended 31 December 20X1

In accordance with our normal practice we set out in this letter certain matters which arose as a result of our review of the accounting systems and procedures operated by your company during our recent audit.

We would point out that the matters dealt with in this letter came to our notice during the conduct of our normal audit procedures which are designed primarily for the purpose of expressing an opinion on the financial statements of your company. In consequence our work did not encompass a detailed review of all aspects of the system and cannot be relied on necessarily to disclose defalcations or to include all possible improvements in internal control.

Present system

No passwords are required to access any part of the computerised accounting system.

Implications

Unrestricted access to the computer system could lead to error, deliberate alteration of accounting records, inefficiency and possible fraud.

Recommendation

Your present software includes the facility to allow restricted access to systems by your staff through a structured system of passwords that can be changed frequently. We recommend that passwords should be introduced as soon as possible.

Present system

Whilst security backup copies of files are taken, these copies are kept in the desk occupied by the accounts clerk.

Implications

Files may be lost or accessed without authorisation.

Recommendation

We recommend that backup files are stored securely in another location.

Proposed system

We noted that you are planning to your offer products for sale via the Internet, and to set up your own website.

Implication

The resulting Internet trading systems may not be compatible with the other computer systems you are currently considering.

Recommendation

We recommend that the development of an Internet trading system should be included within the plans for the general development of your computer systems rather than being tackled as a separate project. Our specialist staff would be pleased to advise you about developing your computer systems. If you want to discuss this further, please contact the audit partner responsible for your affairs.

answers to chapter 5:
ASSESSING RISKS

1   Auditors are required to obtain an understanding of the entity and its environment so that they are able to assess the risks relating to the audit.

2   Audit risk is the risk that the auditors give the wrong opinion on the financial statements. It is made up of three components:

- Inherent risk – risks arising as a result of the nature of the business, its transactions and environment

- Control risk – the risk that the control system at the company does not detect, correct or prevent errors

    (These two risks combined are the risk that errors will exist in the financial statements in the first place)

- Detection risk – the risk that auditors do not discover errors in the financial statements

3   The auditor will take the following steps:

1)   Identify inherent and control risks while obtaining an understanding of the entity
2)   Relate identified risks to what could go wrong at a financial statement level
3)   Consider if the risks are so big they could cause material misstatement
4)   Consider the likelihood of the risk arising
5)   Consider if any of the identified risks are significant risks

4   At a financial statement level:

- Items can be understated or overstated
- Items requiring disclosure can be omitted

5   Materiality is the concept of importance to users. It is relevant to auditors because they will test items which are material.

6   A risk is significant if it is a risk of fraud, a complex transaction, a risk as a result of recent economic or regulatory development, it is a significant transaction with a related party, it has been measured subjectively or it is unusual or appears to be outside the normal course of business for the entity.

7   An auditor needs to obtain sufficient, appropriate evidence. This will be a matter of auditor judgement.

8   The auditors will use the following procedures to obtain evidence about the financial statement assertions (completeness, occurrence, measurement, rights and obligations, existence, accuracy, cut-off, classification/understandability and valuation):

- Enquiry
- Inspection
- Confirmation
- Recalculation
- Analytical procedures

9 and 10

Audit risk	Potential impact on financial statements
Company relies heavily on two customers. One of the customers is currently reviewing Glad Rags to ensure it meets the required qualities of being a quality supplier.	Going concern issues if the company were to lose this custom.
Company relies heavily on the involvement of the sole director, Gladys, who is considering selling the company.	Dominance of an individual director can reduce effectiveness of internal control systems, which could cause error throughout the financial statements. Gladys' plans to sell the company could have implications for going concern, if she does not find a buyer for the company. Gladys' plans to sell the company could lead to a desire to bias the financial statements so that the company looks like a good investment.
The control system is restricted by the low number of administrative staff involved and there appears to be limited segregation of duties in the accounts department.	Lack of segregation of duties can result in errors not being detected by the control systems and therefore arising anywhere in the financial statements. This would cast concern particularly on sales/debtors and purchases/creditors, which are all likely to be material balances.

11   **Items requiring testing**

The following items will require testing because they are above the materiality limit (£70,000):

- Stock
- Debtors
- Creditors falling due in less than one year

However, fixed assets and cash should also be reviewed in case they contain an error of understatement which is material.

12 A key factor which increases the likelihood of error in the financial statements is the fact that the company makes cash sales. This increases the risk of the audit, as turnover is a major and material balance in the financial statements.

Cash is inherently risky because it is easily misappropriated or lost. Greenfingers does have a number of controls over cash sales, but there are also some control problems which adds to the risk that the financial statements may contain an error as a result of problems with cash sales.

13 The following balances are material and should be tested in detail:

- Fixed assets
- Stock
- Trade creditors
- Bank loan

In addition, the bank balance has gone into overdraft which is a major difference from last year. This balance should also be tested in detail, although it is immaterial.

The debtors balance and the accruals balances are immaterial and have not changed significantly from the previous year, therefore it should only be tested by review.

14 Task 1

The main administrative matters that should be covered in the audit strategy are as follows:

(a) The staffing of the audit, indicating what main areas members of the audit team are likely to audit

(b) The arrangements for briefing staff and controlling the audit

(c) The extent to which analyses and summaries can be prepared by the staff of Excellentia plc

(d) The extent of internal audit involvement. The plan should include a summary of the main areas in which the work of internal audit will be used, and how internal audit's work will be reviewed

(e) The extent of involvement by other auditors if they audit any subsidiaries. Details should be given of the arrangements for liaison with other auditors, and how their work will be reviewed

(f) Any areas where the work of an expert will be used as a source of evidence, and the arrangements for reviewing the expert's work

(g) The projected costs of the audit

(h) The timetable for the audit. This should include dates for the interim and final audits, and the date when the accounts are expected to be signed

(i) The stocktaking arrangements. The plan should show that a representative selection of locations, stocks and procedures are to be covered

(j) Arrangements for debtors' and creditors' circularisations if these are to be undertaken

(k) Other administrative details, including arrangements for security of working papers

Task 2

(a) **Liquidity**

It would seem that the liquidity position of the company has declined over the last year. The 'acid test' ratio has reduced from 1.18: 1 (5,200,000: 4,400,000) to just 1.02: 1 (4,800,000: 4,700,000). In the absence of more detailed information, it is impossible to say just how serious this decline in the company's liquidity position is likely to be. The level of bank overdraft has gone up considerably and it appears that a major part of the increase results from the increase in the stock levels held, although this would need to be confirmed by other audit work.

(b) **Tangible fixed assets (tangible non-current assets) and activity**

It is obvious that the tangible fixed assets are a major item in the accounts and that the depreciation charged thereon is a material factor in the determination of profits and losses. The turnover (revenue) has increased in the current year by some 10%, and there has also been an upturn in the level of stocks held, with finished goods stock up by 37.5%. If it transpires that a major part of these increases is the result of inflation, then, especially given the decrease in the level of work in progress, there may well be signs that the plant is not being worked at a full level of capacity.

If this is so, we would need to review carefully management's assessment of asset lives and whether the level of depreciation currently being charged is adequate.

(c) **Sales and debtors (receivables)**

Given that turnover has increased, the fact that debtors have declined seems to be worthy of further investigation. The average number of days sales in debtors at the end of the current year is 63 days as compared with 74 days twelve months earlier (see W1). We should consider the possibility that debtors (and therefore possibly turnover as well) have been understated because of inadequate cut?off procedures (this could also have a bearing on the stock figure) or that they might have been reduced as a result of a significant level of bad debts.

It might also be noted that distribution costs (which are clearly related to sales) are lower this year as a percentage of sales (11.8% compared to 12.5%) and the significance of this can only be seen after further investigation has taken place.

(d) **Stocks (inventory) and activity**

It is possible that the increase in raw materials stocks and the decrease in work in progress are an indication of a reduction in the level of activity (see (b) above), whilst the increase in the level of finished goods stock may be the result of sales falling short of budget.

It should be noted that the gross profit rate has actually increased from 26.7% to 28.6%, possibly suggesting that increased selling prices have resulted in a lower volume of sales. In this connection, it should also be noted that the average number of times that finished stock is turned over in the year has decreased from 4.7 times to 3.6 times. The lower stock turnover should also cause the auditors to consider much more carefully the possibility of a provision for stock obsolescence or deterioration being required.

Working

20X6: $\dfrac{4,800}{28,000}$ x 365 = 63

20X5: $\dfrac{5,200}{25,500}$ x 365 = 74

Task 3

The main computer assisted audit techniques which are used by auditors are the following.

Test data

This comprises data provided by the auditor which is processed by the client's computer system. This may be live data which is processed during the normal systems run or dead test data which is processed outside the normal run. Both valid and invalid data should be processed to ensure rejection controls are operating properly. The purpose of this technique is to test application controls in the system.

Audit software

This comprises computer programs used by the auditor to test the computer files under review and checking in particular the accuracy of the information produced by the company. They run independently of the enterprises' own computer system. Various types of program are available.

15

Financial statement assertion	Example test
Completeness	(a) Review of events after the balance sheet date (b) Cut off (c) Analytical procedures (d) Confirmations (e) Reconciliations to control account (f) Sequence checks (g) Review of reciprocal populations
Rights and obligations	Checking invoices for proof that item belongs to the company Confirmations with third parties
Cut-off	(a) Match up last GRNs with purchase invoices to ensure liability is recorded in the correct period (b) Match up last GRNs with sales invoices to ensure income is recorded in the correct period
Valuation	(a) Checking to invoices (b) Recalculation (c) Confirming accounting policy consistent and reasonable (d) Review of post balance sheet payments and invoices
Existence	(a) Physical verification (b) Third party confirmations (c) Cut off testing
Occurrence	(a) Inspection of supporting documentation (b) Confirmation from directors that transactions relate to business (c) Inspection of items purchased
Accuracy	(a) Re-calculation of correct amounts (b) Third party confirmation (c) Expert valuation (d) Analytical procedures
Classification/ understandability	(a) Check compliance with CA 1985 and SSAPs and FRSs (b) True and fair override invoked

16   Objective   To obtain evidence that items in the profit and loss account are fairly stated.

Work done   Performed analytical procedures on the draft P&L account compared to 20X7. Highlighted variations over 10% where figure for 20X8 is > £20,000.

Results

General comments

1   Decline in trading and profitability was as anticipated due to the recession in the building industry.

2   Some variations should be supported and explained quite easily by our own audit work, eg depreciation in manufacturing costs – refer to fixed asset section; payroll costs to payroll analytical review etc.

3   Other variations require explanations from management and may require further audit work to support the explanation, for example the rise in travelling and entertaining expenses.

Suggested tests

1   Further analysis of turnover (revenue) by month and product line should be carried out to see if there are any unusual factors in the fall, or merely general decline.

2   Similarly, the nature of sales made, that is, the sales mix, should be analysed to see if this reveals why the gross margin has fallen.

3   Director's remuneration should be verified to payroll.

4   Insurance should be verified to policy documents.

5   Legal and other fees should be traced to invoices/correspondence.

6   The audit fee should be verified to our own records.

7   Bank charges should be verified to bank statements.

8   An analysis of the bad debt expense should be obtained and items investigated by discussion with directors and cross-referenced to other debtors' testing.

9   Wages and social security costs should be verified to the payroll.

10   A breakdown of the machine and maintenance balance should be reviewed for reasonableness. We must also ensure no items have been wrongly capitalised in fixed assets (non-current assets).

11   Rent should be verified to the lease agreement.

12   Travelling, entertainment, motor, advertising etc and commission should be verified to invoices. We should ensure the expenses are all business related.

13   Depreciation will be tested as part of the fixed asset (non-current assets) tests.

Conclusion o/s

	£		£
Turnover *	11,536,088	−19	14,315,053
Cost of sales (including manufacturing costs) *	10,271,247	−16	12,260,507
Gross profit	1,264,841		2,054,546
Gross profit % *	11%		14%

	£		£
Administration and establishment charges			
Directors' remuneration *	272,650	+32	206,567
Computer charges	35,410	+3	34,524
Incidental expenses	23,796	−10	26,533
Insurance *	68,992	+38	49,889
Legal and other professional fees *	40,327	+124	18,000
Printing, postage and stationery	24,553	+3	23,817
Repairs and renewals	42,168	+3	41,125
Telephone	28,980	+7	27,153
Depreciation	2,051	−61	5,268
Loss/(profit) on foreign exchange	20,227	n/a	(59,122)
(Profit) on sale of fixed assets	(30,080)	n/a	−
	529,074		373,754
Less: rent received	70,000	0	70,000
	459,074		303,754
% of turnover	4%		2%
	£		£
Finance charges			
Audit *	26,250	+100	13,125
Accountancy	8,750	+67	5,250
Bank charges *	6,024	+8	5,562
Loan interest	33,250	0	33,250
Bad debts *	92,568	+669	13,832
	166,842		71,019
Less: interest received	36,155	−21	45,486
	130,687		25,533
% of turnover	1%		0.2%

	£		£
Manufacturing costs (in cost of sales)			
Wages *	1,938,937	−11	2,180,780
Social Security costs *	193,970	−11	218,120
Machine and maintenance *	37,853	−22	48,311
Light, heat and power	103,995	−9	114,593
Rent *	192,500	+38	140,000
Business rates	11,186	+7	10,444
Hire of machinery	9,958	−47	18,942
Depreciation *	79,683	+88	42,455
Machinery expenses *	25,287	n/a	–
	2,593,369		2,773,645
% of turnover	22%		19%

	£		£
Selling and distribution charges			
Travelling and entertaining expenses *	35,434	+29	27,465
Motor expenses *	35,277	+39	25,326
Depreciation *	62,664	+23	51,089
Advertising and trade fairs *	51,544	+26	40,758
Commission *	5,446	−19	6,751
	190,365		151,389
% of turnover	2%		1%

* = Requires explanation and/or supporting audit work

answers to chapter 6:
AUDIT PLANNING

1   The audit strategy is the overall appraoch for carrying out the audit. The audit plan contains detailed instructions for testing each audit area.

2   **Task 1**

The audit strategy is usually compiled by an audit supervisor or senior. The staff member will usually liaise with the audit partner and manager who might have up-to-date knowledge of the business that the supervisor/ senior otherwise might not have access to. They may also obtain information, such as draft financial statements, from client staff.

Once a supervisor/senior has completed the planning document, they will pass it to the audit manager and partner for review. The audit partner has overall responsibility for the strategy, and will usually hold a planning meeting to ensure all his staff members understand their role on the audit.

Task 2

The audit engagement partner is responsible for overall direction and supervision and review on the audit.

He directs the audit by taking responsibility for audit planning and by choosing the audit team and has meetings with them to ensure that they know what to do. On site, the audit supervisor or senior will direct the work in accordance with the partner's wishes.

Each member of the audit team supervises the work of more junior members of the team.

Similarly, each member of the audit team will review the work of more junior members of the team. The audit manager will conduct a manager's file review and, before the partner gives his opinion on the financial statements, he or she will carry out a partner's file review, to ensure that sufficient evidence has been obtained for him to give his opinion.

3   The audit team will discuss:

- The responsibilities of each audit team member with regard to the audit
- Any issues the audit team should be aware of prior to the audit
- Any confidential issues relevant to the audit
- The auditors' duty of professional scepticism
- The susceptibility of the financial statements to error
- Audit risks

4   The auditors need to consider:

- The professional competence of the expert
- Any professional qualifications of the expert
- The experience of the expert
- The resources of the expert
- The objectivity of the expert

The auditors also need to consider the scope of the expert's work and the actual work that has been done (his sources, when the work was carried out, the results of his work in the context of other audit work carried out).

5   The auditors need to consider how they will co-ordinate with the internal auditors, and ensure that the auditors will have carried out the work that they want to use by the time they want to use it.

6   The key questions to ask are:

–   Does Rozina have the technical competence to perform the internal audit function?

–   Who does she report to – someone suitably independent?

–   Is she accorded sufficient status and authority to make meaningful enquiries, perform tests without restriction etc

–   Is her work properly planned, reviewed and documented?

Spending 2½ days a week on market research should not impugn the validity of Rozina's internal audit work. What you would need to do is to interview her to determine whether she has the knowledge, skills and appropriate attitude to work as an internal auditor. Then you would need to have a look at her work to see if it is up to standard and can be used for external audit purposes.

7   The auditors might use the work of another auditor if they were reporting on the group accounts for which they were not the auditor of one of the subsidiary companies. The auditor would use the work of the auditor of that subsidiary to ensure that there were no matters relating to that subsidiary causing the group accounts not to give a true and fair view.

8   As principal auditors of Big Ted plc we have sole responsibility for our opinion on the group accounts even if part of the group has been audited by others. Therefore we would wish to ensure that we are confident in placing reliance on the work of the auditors of Little Tortoise Ltd (the 'other' auditors).

The Companies Act gives us the right to require that the other auditors give us such information and explanations as we may reasonably require.

As a matter of courtesy we will inform the directors of Big Ted plc of our intention to communicate with the auditors of Little Tortoise Ltd.

The extent of the procedures we will undertake to ensure that we can place reliance on the work of the other auditors will depend on the materiality of the accounts of Little Tortoise Ltd to the group as a whole. We would also need all the relevant information to help us complete the consolidation of Little Tortoise into the group accounts, including details of inter-company trading, inter-company balances at the year end, goodwill, accounting policies and events after the balance sheet date.

We would then consider the scope of the work of Little Tortoise Ltd's auditors. In particular:

(a)   The terms of their engagement and any limitation placed on their work
(b)   The standards of their work and the nature and extent of their audit examination and
(c)   Their independence.

This may be dealt with by meeting the auditors (most appropriate in this first year), by questionnaire or a combination of both. If Little Tortoise Ltd is significant to the group, we may wish to review the other auditors' working papers. In an extreme situation, where we felt we could not rely on the auditors' work we would need to reperform some or all of their work.

9   The auditors must consider that each sampling unit should have an equal chance of being tested. The auditor must be aware that he should not bias the sample, although he must test material items.

10   The following balances were sampled because they were the biggest and therefore gave greatest coverage of the sales ledger.

Affectionado Ltd	76,002
B. Trow Ltd	34,726
Bea Myan Ltd	7,013
Crystal Eyes plc	12,997
Engagement Centre Ltd	16,821
Gemba Gems Ltd	22,032
Gemeyma Ltd	17,152
Love me Tender Ltd	6,111
Ring-ring Ltd	12,142
Wed-Me Ltd	8,429

11   MEMO

To: Jules Devoran
Subject: Audit strategy document

Audit strategy should contain	At Glad Rags
Information obtained as a result of understanding entity and environment procedures	Background information already obtained from previous audits and results of procedures
Materiality set at planning stage	£70,000
Assessment of risks and resulting significant audit areas	Over-reliance on one debtor, potential sale of business, could lead to going concern problems. Potential for bias in overall financial statements to improve chance of sale. Lack of segregation of duties and influence of sole director may compromise control procedures
Audit approach	Largely substantive approach suggested due to inherent problems with control system noted above.
Use of IT	Not being used by auditors
Timing of audit tests	At a final audit
Procedures at yearend	Stocktake attendance Debtors' circularisation
When financial statements should be available	O/s
Audit staff assigned	Audit senior – A Student Audit assistant – J Devoran
Use of other experts/staff	There is no need to use experts and there is no internal audit department at Glad Rags
Other matters	To attend client site Normal Companies Act audit

12   Sample

	£
High value items (above materiality)	
British Clothes Stores plc	484,536
Brodies	74,973
Tisco Stores plc	78,805
Value Mart	323,024
Low value items (below materiality)	
Cavanaghs Limited	14,388
H and T Limited	18,933
Nice Clothes Limited	17,231
Value Clothes Limited	22,315

All items above materiality level were selected as part of the sample. The four lower value items were selected systematically, by selected every 4th items from the remaining list of balances, starting at the third balance (selected haphazardly).

Tutor's note. You should have selected the material items. However, the rest of your sample is unlikely to be the same as this one. Make sure that the reasoning behind your sample selection is correct.

13   The following matters must be included in the audit strategy document:

- Key factors – in particular the risk associated with the business carrying out cash sales

- Planning materiality – £65,000

- Audit approach – given weaknesses in control noted, approach is likely to be highly substantive

- Procedures to carry out at yearend – likely to be confined to stocktake attendance and ensuring bank letter is requested

- Audit staff assigned – myself and Clare

- When final financial statements can be expected – outstanding at this stage, must ask client

- Other administrative details – no specific other points re Greenfingers audit known at this stage

answers to chapter 7:
AUDIT OF STOCKS

1 The stock count (sometimes called a stocktake).

2 If stock cut-off is incorrect, assets may be double counted in the financial statements, or assets may be counted without a corresponding liability.

For example, if the company record a sale but the stock is also counted as existing at the yearend, then the company has two assets in the financial statements (stock and debtor, and a sale) whereas, if they have sold the stock, they should not still be counting the asset of the stock.

To give another example, if the company accept goods on the day of the stocktake, which get counted into the count, but do not record the invoice in purchases until the following year, then the company has an asset in the financial statements (stock) which does not have the relevant liability and expense recorded (purchases/creditor).

In both cases, profit is overstated, in sales and closing stock in the first case and in closing stock with no corresponding purchase in the second case.

3 The auditors will need to verify:

- The initial cost of the raw materials (usually tested by reference to original purchase invoices)

- The cost of conversion to finished goods (for example, labour costs, usually tested by reference to time records and the payroll, and overhead costs, usually tested by reference to overall overhead costs and the invoices for these costs)

4 In individual cases, the auditors should verify items to post-year end sales or sales information (for example, price catalogue) to ensure that the cost valuation is lower than net realisable value.

The auditors should also carry out the following general tests:

- Ensuring stock which appeared damaged at the stocktake has been valued accordingly

- Examine sales prices after the year to ensure that none have significantly dropped (perhaps to below cost)

- Review quantities of stock sold after the yearend to ensure that goods are not obsolescent

- Consider whether adjustments are required for slow-moving goods

5   Stocktake – key issues

Jules should review the stocktaking instructions and my comments below and ensure that the stocktake is carried out in accordance with them.

Jules should test-check some of the counts that the checkers have made. Last year's sample was 12. As Joe Worple has stated that there are no major changes in stock this year, the same sample size should be used.

Jules should focus his attention on raw materials, which is likely to be a higher amount in total than finished goods. In particular, he should ensure that he includes within his count the specialist fabric A001, and the major stock lines of S01, CJ02 and CJ03. Given that the stores manager has said there are no major changes in stock, these items should be high value as they were last year.

However, he should also select some finished goods within the sample as the overall value of finished goods may be higher than raw materials, although the quantity is smaller and ensure that, as instructed, no work in progress exists.

Jules should remeasure some items during the count to ensure that the controls over amount of fabric operate effectively. I suggest an initial sample of 5 bales. He should also review a sample of the records on the bales to ensure that they are arithmetically accurate.

The main count will be taking place in the stores, so Jules should meet Mr Worple there. However, he should also ensure that he attends the machine room at 3pm to ensure that all operations have finished before the count starts.

Lastly, Jules should obtain details of the last delivery from the factory and the last delivery to the factory before the stocktake to enable stock cut off tests to be carried out at the final audit.

Review of stocktaking instructions

The stocktaking instructions show that the count has been well thought out and appears organised. There are good controls over checks and to ensure that items are not counted twice. Controls to prevent movements of stock during the count appear to be sound. Provided the count is carried out according to the instructions, the count should be capable of providing a suitable figure for stock existence.

The key control is the existing control over quantity of stock, which is that the bales are marked down for fabric removed and most of it is not remeasured at the stock count. We must be satisfied that this control is operating effectively to be able to rely on the count. Therefore it is important to check both that the record attached to the stock tallies with the amount of stock present and that the records are arithmetically accurate.

6

Client:	Glad Rags Ltd	Prepared by:	J Devoran
Accounting date:	30 November 20X4	Date:	2 January 20X5
		Reviewed by:	A Student
		Date:	11 January 20X5

Stock cut off

Last deliveries out

Sales order/GDN	Customer	Agreed to November Sales Day Book
200894/DN12403	Value Mart	✓
200895/DN12404	BCS	✓
200896/DN12405	Tisco Stores	✓

The above items have all been excluded from the stock count

Last deliveries in (from invoices pending file - these were the only three orders received pending invoices)

Order	Supplier	Agreed to November Purchase Day Book
P1013	Fine Fabrics Ltd	✓
P1017	Fine Fabrics Ltd	✓
P1021	Terry's Threads	*

* This invoice was not received until 15 December and was included in December's Purchase Day Book. The value was £2,476.

All the above items were included in the stock count.

Conclusion

Sales cut off is correct.

An error was discovered in purchase cut off. One invoice, value £2,476, was included in December purchases in error. This is not material, but should be included on a schedule of non-material potential adjustments. As the item was correctly included in stock, the adjustment to the financial statements would be:

		£	£
Dr	Purchases	2,476	
Cr	Trade creditors		2,476

As the company does not maintain goods received records, it is impossible to check whether this mistake is isolated. However, given that every order received pending invoice was checked, if we are satisfied that the existing controls over orders received are satisfactory, we should be able to rely that this error is isolated, and that, subject to the adjustment above, purchases cut off is fairly stated.

The failure of the company to keep goods received records is a weakness that we should include in a management letter.

7 Jules – To complete the work you have started on stock existence, you need to trace the items you test counted at the stock take to the final stocksheets that were prepared to produce the overall audit figure for stock to ensure that they were included properly in the final figure for stock.

8

Client:	Glad Rags Ltd	Prepared by:	A Student
Accounting date:	30 November 20X4	Date:	11 January 20X5
		Reviewed by:	
		Date:	

Stock valuation

Objective: To ensure that stock is valued at the lower of cost and net realisable value

Work done: Raw materials cost verified to purchase invoice cost. Finished goods verified to catalogue costs to ensure that they are valued lower than net realisable value.

Raw materials

Stock code	Description	Quantity	Unit cost	Value	Cost correct?
A001	Special fabric	200m	6.00	1,200	Yes
CJ03	Cotton jersey – blue	221m	1.20	265	Yes
N01	Nylon – white	135m	1.25	169	Yes

Finished goods

Stock code	Description	Quantity	Unit cost	Value	Lower than NRV?
Z111	Babygros white	1,000	5.35	5,350	Yes
X102	T-shirts red	2,000	3.10	6,200	Yes
X204	BMC skirts – red	12,000	10.00	120,000	Yes

Conclusion: Raw materials are valued correctly. It will be necessary to perform further work on finished goods to establish whether they are valued correctly. The items selected are valued at lower than net realisable value, but work will need to be done to ascertain whether the cost of finished goods is correct. We will need to determine what how the cost is determined (raw materials costs/labour costs/any production overheads) and verify these to the appropriate items (purchase invoices/payroll and time records/overhead cost invoices).

9   Task 1

The work I will carry out before the start of the stocktake will be as follows.

(a)   Review previous year's audit working papers and discuss any developments in the year with management.

(b)   Obtain and review a copy of the company's stocktaking instructions.

(c)   Arrange attendance at stock count planning meetings, with the consent of management.

(d)   Gain an understanding of the nature of the stock and of any special stocktaking problems this is likely to present, for example scrap in piles.

(e)   Consider whether specialist involvement is likely to be required as a result of any circumstances noted in (d) above.

(f)   Using the results of the above steps, plan for audit attendance by appropriately experienced audit staff.

(g)   Consider the impact of internal control upon the nature and timing of the stocktaking attendance.

(h)   Discuss with management the extent to which each stockline is considered complete at each stage of the manufacturing process.

Task 2

The stock-taking instructions should cover the following procedures:

(a)   Supervision of the planning and execution of the stocktake by sufficient senior and qualified personnel drawn from various departments: at least some of the officials should not normally be involved with the custody of stocks.

(b)   Tidying and marking stock to facilitate counting of items of stock. The whole of the stocktaking area should be divided into sections for control purposes.

(c)   The serial numbering and control of the issue and return of all the rough count records, and their retention as required by the Companies Act.

(d)   Systematic carrying out of counts to ensure coverage of the whole stock.

(e)   Arrangements for the count to be conducted by at least two people, with one counting and the other primarily to check the count, or alternatively for two independent counts to be carried out; and for any differences arising to be investigated and resolved.

(f)   Stock sheets being completed in ink and being signed by those who carried out and checked the count.

(g)   Information to be recorded on the count records. (Normally this will include the location and identity of the stock items, the unit of count, the quantity counted, the condition of the items and the stage reached in the production process.)

(h)   Restriction and control of the production process and stock movements during the count.

(i)   Identification and segregation of damaged, obsolete, slow moving, third parties' stocks and returnable stocks, so that these can be properly accounted for and recorded.

(j)   Recording the quantity, condition and stage of production of all the work in progress for subsequent checking with the costing and stock records.

(k)   Co-ordination of the count with cut off procedures so that documentation concerned with the flow of goods can be reconciled with the financial records. For this purpose, last numbers of goods inwards and outward records and of internal transfer records should be noted.

(l)   Reconciliation with the stock records, if any, and identification and correction of differences.

Task 3

The following work should be carried out at the stocktake:

(a)   Carry out a series of test counts between the stock and the count records and vice-versa. Attention should be given to high value stocks.

(b)   Obtain information about the stock's condition, age, usage and, in the case of work in progress, its stage of completion.

(c) In order to ensure that stock cut-off is correct, the following procedures should be carried out.

 (i) Make a record during the stocktaking attendance of all movement notes relating to the period, including:

  (1) All inter-departmental requisition numbers
  (2) The last goods received note and despatch note prior to the count
  (3) The first goods received note and despatch note after the count

 (ii) Observe whether correct cut-off procedures are being followed in the despatch and receiving areas. Discuss procedures with company staff performing the count to ensure they are understood.

 (iii) Ensure that no goods finished on the day of the count are transferred to the warehouse.

(d) Finally the auditors should:

 (i) Conclude whether the stocktaking has been properly carried out and is sufficiently reliable as a basis for determining the existence of stock

 (ii) Consider whether any amendment is necessary to their subsequent audit procedures

 (iii) Try to gain from their observations an overall impression of the levels and values of stocks held so that they may, in due course, judge whether the figure for stocks appearing in the financial statements is reasonable

Task 4

During the final audit, the auditors will use the cut-off information from the stocktake to perform the following procedures.

(a) Match up the last goods received notes with purchase invoices and ensure the liability has been recorded in the correct period. Only goods received before the year end should be recorded as purchases.

(b) Match up the last goods despatched notes to sales invoices and ensure the income has been recorded in the correct period. Only stocks despatched before the year end should be recorded as sales.

(c) Match up the requisition notes to the work in progress details for the receiving department to ensure correctly recorded.

Task 5

Stock which may be worth less than cost will include:

- Slow moving stock
- Obsolete stock
- Seconds stock and items that have been damaged
- Stock which is being, or is soon likely to be, sold at reduced prices
- Discontinued stock lines

To identify stock which may be worth less than cost the following work should be carried out:

(a)   Examine the computerised stock control system and list items showing an unacceptably low turnover rate. An unacceptable rate of turnover may be different for different items, but stock representing more than three months sales is likely to qualify in a business with a rapidly changing market.

(b)   Check the stock printout for items already described as seconds or recorded as damaged. Some of these should agree with my own observations at the stocktake, but should be more comprehensive.

(c)   Discuss with management the current position regarding slow moving stock and their plans and expectations in respect of products that may be discontinued. Estimates must be obtained of the likely selling price of existing stock. The trade press would be a good place to check prices.

(d)   At the stocktake, stock should have been noted which was dusty, inaccessible and in general not moving and marked as such on the stock sheets.

(e)   Find out (by examining repair report sheets etc) whether any lines are unreliable and therefore frequently returned for repairs as these may be unpopular and impossible to sell in future. (Note. They may be returnable to the supplier at full purchase cost under warranty.)

(f)   Check with the trade press or other sources to see whether any of the stock is out of date. The computer business involves rapidly changing technology and fashions and so stock (inventory) could easily be out of date and unsaleable.

(g)   Look at the audit file from last year and consider any items which were investigated then to see if NRV was less than cost. Any such items still in stock a year later may be worth very little.

(h)   Question sales, warehouse and technical staff at the client as to whether any stock is very slow moving or selling at less than cost.

(i)   As part of the review of board minutes, management reports, and sales literature, look for references to sales, price cuts, promotions, slow moving stock etc.

(j)   Check to see whether new models of products have been introduced, making predecessor models less attractive and therefore less valuable.

(k)   Look at customer returns of faulty/damaged products around the year end. Discuss with engineers whether the stock will be repaired and returned to the customer or scrapped.

(l)   Check sales prices at the year end, looking in particular for large discounts offered on certain lines, or lower prices charged than before the year end. In particular, check high-value items of stock as the over-valuation of such stock could have a significant impact on the company's results.

answers to chapter 8:
AUDIT OF OTHER ASSETS (AND RELATED ITEMS)

1   **Audit tests over fixed asset completeness**

- Obtain a summary of fixed assets and reconcile with the opening position (additions and disposals)

- Compare fixed assets in the general ledger with the fixed asset register and obtain explanations for any differences

- Check that assets which physically exist are included in the register

2   The auditor will consider:

- Cost
- Whether the asset has been revalued and when
- Depreciation (whether it is reasonable/whether it has been calculated correctly)

3

Client: Kandistors Limited		Prepared by:	
Year-end: 31 December 20X3		Reviewed by:	
Subject: Fixed Assets		Date:	Date:
Objective	**Test**		**Completed by**
Completeness	1	Ensure **opening balances** in **accounting records agree** to **last year's accounts**.	
	2	**Check** that the **assets seen** at the client's **premises** have been **recorded** in **the fixed asset register**.	
	3	**Compare** the **fixed asset register** with the **fixed asset accounts** in the ledger, and check that **differences in value** can be **satisfactorily explained**.	
	4	**Review repairs, maintenance** and **sundry expenditure** during the year, and **enquire** into **any expenditure** that looks as if it should have been **capitalised**.	
	5	Compare **actual fixed asset expenditure** with **budgeted expenditure** and **obtain explanations** for differences.	
	6	**Check** that all **fixed asset expenditure** shown as authorised in the board minutes has been made.	
Existence	1	**Inspect a sample of assets** that are **recorded** in the **fixed asset register**.	
	2	**Examine invoices, MOT records** and other independent documentary evidence of assets' existence.	
	3	**Examine invoices** for **smaller furniture and equipment additions** to see if any have been **incorrectly capitalised**.	
Ownership	1	**Inspect title deeds** for land and buildings.	
	2	**Inspect other documentation** (vehicle registration documents, insurance policies) for evidence of title to other assets.	
	3	Inspect **purchase invoices**, records of **assets received** and **solicitors' completion statements** for **assets purchased** during the year to see if they are in the client's name and purchases have been properly authorised.	
	4	**Review bank letter** for details of assets and title documents held.	
Valuation	1	When inspecting assets, note any **signs of undue wear** or **lack of use**.	
	2	**Examine purchase invoices** for evidence of costs of assets purchased during the year.	
Classification/ understand- ability	1	**Check** that the **presentation** of **fixed assets** in the accounts is in **accordance with legislation** and accounting standards.	
	2	**Check** that the **accounting policies** that relate to **fixed assets** have been **clearly disclosed**.	

4   The auditor must not neglect:

- Material balances
- Old unpaid accounts
- Credit balances
- Zero balances
- Accounts which have been paid by the date of examination

5   There is usually a great deal of analytical information about sales (for example, analyses of sales per month or per product) at a company, and sales has a number of predictable relationships (with debtors, with gross margin) so it is a good balance to test by analytical procedures.

6   Auditors should send out a bank letter request two weeks before the company's year end.

7   Window dressing is the practice of manipulating when cash receipts and payments are recorded and sent out to manipulate balance sheet results at the yearend.

For example, if a company wanted liabilities to look lower, then it might record a number of payments (which would also therefore be included on the bank reconciliation, reducing the bank balance) but not physically send those cheques out until after the yearend, so that in practice, the bank balance is higher than it appears to be in the accounts, as is the creditor balance.

8

Client:	Glad Rags Ltd	Prepared by:	A Student
Accounting date:	30 November 20X4	Date:	19 January 20X5
		Reviewed by:	
		Date:	

Debtors circularisation

Objective: To ensure that debtors exist and are genuine obligations to the company

Work done: Debtors replies reconciled to sales ledger balances. Where replies not available, cash received after date gives sufficient evidence concerning existence and rights.

Debtor	Balance per sales ledger £	Agreed to debtor reply	Comments/reconciliation	Balance Agreed?
BCS	484,536	No	Difference is a receipt for £44,938 in December cashbook	o/s *
Brodies	74,973	Yes	–	Yes
Tisco Stores	78,805	No	Difference is requested credit note for 1107, re SI-12950	o/s**
Value Mart	323,024	Yes	–	Yes
Cavanaghs	14,388	Yes	–	Yes
H and T	18,933	N/A	Balance agreed to cash receipts in Dec and Jan total £18,933	Yes
Nice Clothes	17,231	N/A	Balance agreed to cash receipts in Dec and Jan total £17,231	Yes
Value Clothes	22,315	Yes	–	Yes

Further work required

* We should review this receipt further and determine when it was received by the company, as it does not appear in the cashbook until a week after it was sent by the customer. It may be that this receipt should actually be included in the year. However, as Glad Rags does not retain customer remittances, it may not be possible to determine the correct timing of this receipt.

** We should discuss this requested credit with the sales department and discover whether the goods were returned. This may have implications for stock if the goods are damaged but were counted in the stock count. If a credit is justified, this credit note should be reserved and the debt reduced.

Conclusion

Subject to the points made above, existence and rights to debtors appears to be stated fairly.

9 Audit of valuation of debtors

Jules

Valuation of debts can be tested by scrutinising the cash paid subsequent to the year end. Auditors will be particularly concerned with older debts on the ledger, especially when subsequent debts have been paid, as this may indicate that the old debt is not likely to be paid and has therefore been overvalued.

You should do the following:

1) Obtain a aged debt analysis from the sales ledger at 30 November

2) Scrutinise it to identify debts greater than 60 days old at 30 November (60 days being the standard payment period of Glad Rags' debtors)

3) Review the cash book for evidence of the old debts being paid

4) If some old debts are still unpaid as at the middle of January, they must be discussed with the accountant to assess whether action has been taken

5) Scrutinise any correspondence with the late payer

6) Consider any allowance made for bad debts and assess whether it is sufficient

7) Identify any further adjustments that might need to be made in respect of bad debts and write them on the schedule of unadjusted errors (unless they are material – in which case you should bring them to my attention immediately)

10 **Tests to be carried out on fixed assets at Greenfingers:**

Completeness

- Compare fixed assets in the general ledger with the fixed asset register and reconcile any differences

- Select a sample of assets which physically exist and trace them to the fixed asset register

- Review sensitive balances in the profit and loss account (such as repairs or motor costs) to ensure items which should have been capitalised have not been expensed in the year

Rights and obligations

- Review title deeds for land and buildings
- Check a sample of registration documents for company vehicles

Existence

- Select a sample of assets from the fixed asset register and trace the physical assets
- Inspect the assets to ensure they exist, and are in good condition and use

Valuation

As assets have not been revalued, focus valuation testing on additions.

- Check the purchase invoices for the new vehicles and fittings
- Review depreciation rates to ensure they are reasonable
- Recalculate depreciation to ensure it has been correctly calculated
- Ensure value of major land and buildings assets has not been impaired

11

Client:	Greenfingers Limited	Prepared by:	A Student
Accounting date:	31 December 20X4	Date:	8 May 20X5
		Reviewed by:	
		Date:	

Analytical procedures: Sales

Objective: To ascertain the truth and fairness of the sales figure in the financial statements.

Work done: Analytical review performed on sales and profit analysis provided by client.

SALES

		Shop 1	Shop 2 (75% of Shop 1)	Shop 3 (65% of Shop 1)	Café (1/2 shop 1 customers)	Conclusion
High (Apr – Jul)	Customers Days* Income	400 × 30.5 × 30 **£366,000**	**£274,500**	**£237,900**	200 × 30.5 × 8 **£48,800**	Sales analysis shows sales to be in this range.
Mid (Feb/Mar Aug/Sept)	Customers Days Income	300 × 30.5 × 20 **£183,000**	**£137,250**	**£118,950**	150 × 30.5 × 8 **£36,600**	Sales analysis shows sales to be in this range.
Low (Oct – Jan)	Customers Days Income	200 × 30.5 × 15 **£91,500**	**£68,625**	**£59,475**	100 × 30.5 × 8 **£24,400**	Sales analysis shows sales to be in this range.

*Note: a rough average of 30.5 days per month has been used.

PROFIT

		Shop 1	Shop 2	Shop 3	Café	Conclusion
Total sales	6,656,013	2,590,000	1,942,500	1,683,500	440,013	The gross margins for the
Gross profit		815,850	611,888	530,303	264,008	shops and the café are as
Gross profit margin	GP/Sales × 100	31.5%	31.5%	31.5%	60%	are expected.

Conclusion: Sales and gross margins appear to be fairly stated.

12

BANK RECONCILIATION			
31 December 20X4			
			£
Balance per cashbook		CB	(17,000)
Less: 31 Dec takings		✓4.1*	(1,278)
Add: Cheque payments	003465	✓6.1	5,398
	003466	✓6.1	2,476
	003467	✓6.1	15,398
	003468	✓5.1	108
	003469	✓10.1	2,365
	003470	✓7.1	3,465
	003471	✓5.1	791
	003472	✓5.1	23
Balance per bank statement		B	11,746
			^

Key:
B – agreed to bank letter
CB – agreed to cashbook
✓ date – agreed to bank statements
* = 884 + 394
^ = adds correctly

13   **Task 1**

Client:	Tiffenies	
A/c Date:	31 March 20X2	
Prepared by:	ME	Date: 5 June 20X2
Reviewed by:	Date:	

Debtors' circularisation results

The debtors' circularisation has confirmed £12,081 directly, while another balance of £2,611 has been reconciled to the ledger. This totals £14,692, or 36.6% of the sample, 24% of total debtors.

As the results of the debtors' circularisation have historically been poor, and there is evidence of debtors paying balances subsequent to the year end, no follow up of debtors will be undertaken.

Instead, the remaining sample of debtors' balances will be agreed where possible to cash received after date. As the majority of cash receipts tie in to invoice batches in the sales ledger records, this is a good secondary method of gaining evidence about debtors.

Task 2

Client:	Tiffenies				H22

A/c Date:	31 March 20X2			

Prepared by: ME   Date: 5 June 20X2

Reviewed by: Date:

Debtors: after cash confirmation

A/c code	Name	Balance	Cash received (per CB)	Date	Details
		£	£		
AND01	Andropov	1,567	630	31.5.X2	Pays oldest
BAK02	Baker and Co	3,487	1,238	2.4.X2	Pays Jan
			1,157	7.5.X2	Pays Feb
PEA01	Peacock & Lorenzo	3,124	3,124	3.4.X2	ALL PAID
TAB02	Table Partnership	1,204	174	2.4.X2	X-ref to H21
TRA01	Transnational	12,045	NONE		X-ref to H2
AIM	Zaidi	3,994	1,477	12.4.X2	Pays Feb

Task 3

Client: Tiffenies
A/c date: 31.3.20X2
Prepared by: ME   Date: 6.6.X2
Reviewed by   Date:

Management letter points

Two significant points arise:

Credit limits

Weakness

A large number of debtors on the ledger had balances larger than their credit limit at 31 March 20X2.

Consequence

Extending credit above a pre-determined credit limit increases the chance of debt becoming bad and not being paid.

Recommendation

Tiffenies should reassess the credit limits they apply to customers. If, in the light of the trading history between the parties, they feel that the current credit limit is unrealistic, they should amend their credit limits. If not, they should ensure that they do not extend credit to customers who have reached their limit.

Credit control

Weaknesses

A number of debtors on the ledger also appear to have been extended a credit period in excess of Tiffenies' stated credit terms. In addition to this, the credit controller appears only to chase a due debt when it has been outstanding for twice the length of time that it should have been.

Consequence

It is possible that Tiffenies could be extending excessive credit to customers who are unable to pay, in which case Tiffenies are increasing the loss that would be due to them. The credit limits and periods have been set for a purpose, which is to minimise potential loss to the company, while retaining common business practice.

Recommendation

Tiffenies should encourage customers to pay within the credit terms, by sending customers statements on a monthly basis, showing the debt due, and by chasing debt at 60 days, when it falls due.

Task 4

Client:	Tiffenies		
A/c date:	31.3.X2		
Prepared by:	ME		Date: 6.6.X2
Reviewed by:			Date:

Memorandum: points arising from audit of debtors

(a) **Work done**

A debtors' circularisation was undertaken and the results analysed at the final audit stage. Three debtors agreed the balance stated, and two further replied with a disagreement as to the balance. These two balances have now been reconciled. There appears to have been a cut off error with credit notes, on which further work should be undertaken (see below, point b(ii)).

This means that half of the debtors circularised did not respond. However, as the response rate to circularisation has historically been poor, these were not followed up, and the remaining balances were tested in relation to after date cash received.

The results of the after date cash review show that, while not all the balance outstanding at March has now been paid off, with one exception (see below, point b(i)), the oldest debt on the ledger has been paid off. It seems fair to conclude, subject to the point below, that the debtors' ledger is fairly stated.

(b) **Further work required**

(i) **Transnational**

The debt from Transnational is the largest debt sampled and it has now been outstanding for 6 months. It consists of two invoices from mid-December. This implies that it may have been an event in connection with Christmas.

This debt should be discussed with the credit controller. We need to determine whether this is a one off account, or whether the client has a history with the customer. It might be that Tiffenies always do work for Transnational at Christmas, and they never pay until July.

If this is a one off account, it may be worth our re-circularising Transnational, as this in itself may remind them to pay the debt, as well as providing audit evidence. We may also need to discuss the need for Tiffenies to take legal advice in respect of this debt.

If it appears that the debt has turned bad, after further audit work has been carried out, we should suggest that the directors write off the debt in the financial statements, as this amount is material to the debtor balance.

(ii) **Credit notes**

It appears that there may have been a cut off problem with credit notes in the sales ledger prior to year end, as two of the reconciling items on H21 were pre-year end credit notes.

We should undertake a review of credit notes to ensure that these problems are isolated.

Again, this may require an adjustment to be made to the financial statements.

(c) **Points arising**

(i) **Circularisation**

Historically the response rate to this exercise has been poor, so it is important to consider whether it is worth carrying out a debtors' circularisation in future years.

However, the circularisation provides good audit evidence, and 50% of debtors sampled responded this year, which is a fair response rate.

(ii) **Bad debt**

If further work reveals that the debt to Transnational is bad, then the financial statements should be adjusted to reflect this. If the directors refused to amend the financial statements over this issue, then we might have to qualify the audit opinion on the grounds of disagreement over this issue. This would be an 'except for' qualification.

answers to chapter 9:
AUDIT OF LIABILITIES
(AND RELATED ITEMS)

1   Supplier statements

2   When internal controls over purchases are weak, or when the auditor suspects that the trade creditors balance has been understated.

3   The auditor will trace a sample of items from initial records (such as purchase requisitions) through the system to the nominal ledger, to ensure that they have been included correctly in the final accounts.

4   ■   Check that accruals are fairly calculated

   ■   Verify accruals by reference to subsequent payments

   ■   Review profit and loss account and prior years to consider whether other accruals are required

5   Bank loans and debentures

6   ■   Obtain/prepare a schedule of loans outstanding at the balance sheet date

   ■   Compare opening balances to the previous year's working papers (closing balances at the end of last year)

   ■   Test the clerical accuracy of the schedule

   ■   Compare balances to the general ledger

   ■   Check the names of lenders to relevant information (such as bank letter or register of debentureholders)

   ■   Review minutes and cashbook to ensure that all loans have been recorded

7   **Objective**

   To obtain evidence that creditors are not materially understated.

   Work done

   Using the suppliers' statement summaries, the following reconciliations have been prepared.

Results

Wembley Wheels Ltd

Balance per supplier	15,500
Balance per purchase ledger	15,500

Account reconciled

Mitchells Classic Oils Ltd

Balance per supplier	6,800
Less: payment not on supplier statement	1,550
Balance per purchase ledger	5,250

Account reconciled

Patel Engine Parts Ltd

Balance per supplier	37,600
Less: payment not on supplier statement	5,000
Less: discount taken not allowed by supplier	200
Less: invoice 1812 not recorded	5,200
Balance per purchase ledger	27,200

Account reconciled

Helga Auto Parts Ltd

Balance per supplier	25,890
Balance per purchase ledger	25,890

Account reconciled

Leather Seats Ltd

Balance per supplier	9,818
Less: invoice 12297 not recorded	4,598
Less: payment not on supplie r statement	5,220
Balance per purchase ledger	NIL

Account reconciled

Conclusion. From the sample extracted, creditors are understated by £9,798 in total. This is made up of the two unrecorded invoices, no 1812 from Patel Engine Parts for £5,200 and no 12297 from Leather Seats Ltd. for £4,598. Additional testing is required using a larger sample.

Adjustment required. Dr Purchases (cost of sales) £9,798, Cr Purchase Ledger Control Account £9,798.

8   The question suggests that suppliers might be slow in submitting their invoices and therefore there may be year-end cut off problems.

Response to task 1

The key audit objective or assertion is that of completeness, ie all relevant liabilities are recorded.

An element of validity also applies to ensure that liabilities relating to the new year are not recorded in the books for the current year under review.

Response to task 2

A standard purchase cut off test would be to take a sample of goods received notes for an appropriate period before the year end and after the year end and trace these to suppliers' invoices and creditors records to confirm that the relevant liabilities are taken up in the correct year.

9

Client:	Glad Rags Ltd	Prepared by:	A Student
Accounting date:	30 November 20X4	Date:	20 January 20X5
		Reviewed by:	
		Date:	

Supplier statement reconciliation

Objective: To ensure that amounts owed by the company are genuine and valued correctly

Work done: Sample of purchase ledger balances reconciled to supplier statements

Supplier	Balance per ledger	Balance per statement	Reconciling items	Balance agreed?
AA	387	387	–	Yes
Fine	102,486	102,486	–	Yes
Terry's	97,429	100,375	Credit note not included on the supplier's statement	Yes
Fabric Wholesaler	112,462	112,462	–	Yes

Conclusion

Trade creditors are fairly stated

10 **Sample**

The following balances are material and must be sampled:

Dawsons Fencing Limited:	£75,003
Very Nice Garden Company Limited:	£89,035

(Note: Remember that materiality is £65,000.)

Work to be carried out on trade creditors

■   Check that the purchase ledger list of balances adds correctly

■   Ensure that the general ledger and purchase ledger list of balances total agree

■   Sample of creditors to be verified to supplier statements

■   Differences between ledger and statements to be investigated and reconciled (payments/ credit notes/invoices etc)

11 The accruals balance is immaterial and has not changed significantly from the previous year, so does not need to be tested in detail.

The list of accruals should be compared to the previous year to see whether it appears reasonable. If the lists are significantly different, the accruals balance may need to be tested in more detail. The auditors should also consider the expenses of the business and consider whether any other accruals are likely to be necessary.

answers to chapter 10: AUDIT COMPLETION AND REPORTING

1   Post balance sheet events

1) Outcome of legal action commenced prior to the yearend
2) Customer going into liquidation
3) New commitments or borrowings

2   After the audit report has been signed, the directors are responsible for drawing relevant subsequent events to the auditors' attention. However, the auditors are still required to state whether the financial statements give a true and fair view, so subsequent events after the original audit report may give rise to a new audit report being required, if the directors change the financial statements, or if they don't and a true and fair view is no longer given.

3   They should consider whether this is a limitation of scope on their audit requiring them to give a qualified opinion. They should also consider whether the directors' refusal to sign a letter of representation casts doubt on other representations the directors have made to them during the course of the audit.

4   The basic elements of the audit report

- A title, identifying to whom the audit report is addressed

- Addressee (normally the shareholders)

- An introductory paragraph, indicating the financial statements being audited

- A statement of management's responsibility for the financial statements

- A statement of the auditor's responsibility

- Scope paragraph including a description of the work performed by the auditor (basis of audit opinion)

- Opinion paragraph

- Auditor's address and signature of the auditors

- Date of the signature

5   If the auditors had a disagreement with the directors about something in the financial statements which they felt was pervasive to those financial statements, meaning that a true and fair view was not given by the financial statements.

6 The four possible types of opinion where there are matters that affect the auditor's opinion are:

    (a) **Qualified opinion: limitation on scope (except for ... might)**

    This qualified opinion is given where there has been a limitation on scope in the auditors' work in one area. It is not considered to be fundamental but the auditor cannot give an opinion on it. Therefore they issue an unqualified report except in the area where their work was limited.

    (b) **Disclaimer of opinion**

    This opinion is given where the limitations on the scope of the auditors' work are so great that they cannot give an opinion on the truth and fairness of the financial statements.

    (c) **Qualified opinion: disagreement (except for)**

    This qualified opinion is given where the auditors disagree with the treatment or disclosure of one item in the accounts which is not considered fundamental. They issue an unqualified report except in the area they disagree with.

    (d) **Adverse opinion**

    This opinion is given where the auditors disagree with the treatment or disclosures in the financial statements so much that they do not believe that the financial statements give a true and fair view.

7 **Task 1**

Signs are as follows:

Financial

    (a) An excess of liabilities over assets

    (b) Net current liabilities

    (c) Necessary borrowing facilities have not been agreed

    (d) Default on terms of loan agreements, and potential breaches of covenant

    (e) Significant liquidity or cash flow problems

    (f) Major losses or cash flow problems which have arisen since the balance sheet date and which threaten the entity's continued existence

    (g) Substantial sales of fixed assets (non-current assets) not intended to be replaced

    (h) Major restructuring of debts

    (i) Denial of (or reduction in) normal terms of trade credit by suppliers

    (j) Major debt repayment falling due where refinancing is necessary to the entity's continued existence

    (k) Inability to pay debts as they fall due

Operational

(a) Fundamental changes to the market or technology to which the entity is unable to adapt adequately

(b) Externally forced reductions in operations (for example, as a result of legislation or regulatory action)

(c) Loss of key management or staff, labour difficulties or excessive dependence on a few product lines where the market is depressed

(d) Loss of key suppliers or customers or technical developments which render a key product obsolete

Other

(a) Major litigation in which an adverse judgement would imperil the entity's continued existence

(b) Issues which involve a range of possible outcomes so wide that an unfavourable result could affect the appropriateness of the going concern basis

Task 2

The main procedures that should be used to identify material events after the balance sheet date are as follows:

(a) Enquire into, and consider the effectiveness of, the procedures management has established to ensure that subsequent events are identified.

(b) Read minutes of the meetings of members, the board of directors and audit and executive committees held after the period end.

(c) Enquire about matters discussed at meetings for which minutes are not yet available.

(d) Review relevant accounting records and read the entity's latest available financial information, such as interim financial statements, budgets, cash flow forecasts and other related management reports.

(e) Make enquires of management as to whether any subsequent events have occurred which might affect the financial statements.

Task 3

In certain cases, such as:

(a) Where knowledge of the facts is confined to management
(b) Where the matter is principally one of judgement and opinion

the auditors may not be able to obtain independent corroborative evidence and could not reasonably expect it to be available. In such cases, the auditors should ensure that there is no other evidence which conflicts with the representations made by management and they should obtain written confirmation of the representations.

Where written representations are obtained, the auditors will still need to decide whether in the circumstances these representations, together with such other audit evidence as they have obtained, are sufficient to enable them to form an opinion on the financial statements. The letter of representation has various subsidiary purposes:

(a)   To confirm the directors' responsibilities for the financial statements

(b)   To confirm that the financial records reflect all the transactions of the company and that all information has been made available to the auditors

(c)   To confirm in writing any oral representations made by management

(d)   To highlight any matters of importance which need to be disclosed in the financial statements

If the directors are still not prepared to sign the letter then we must consider their position. The letter of representation is part of the audit evidence. Failure to obtain a letter will result in us reviewing the audit evidence we have obtained through other means for the matters dealt with in the letter. Where this evidence is not sufficient, we may need to qualify our audit opinion.

8

Client:	Glad Rags Ltd	Prepared by:	J Devoran
Accounting date:	30 November 20X4	Date:	21 January 20X5
		Reviewed by:	
		Date:	

Overall review of financial statements

Objective: To ensure that the financial statements appear to be consistent within t hemselves.

Work done: Financial statement ratios carried out.

Ratios		*2003*
$\dfrac{\text{Gross profit}}{\text{Turnover}} \times 100$	$\dfrac{2{,}121{,}814}{7{,}103.495} \times 100 = 29.87\%$	(30.2%)
$\dfrac{\text{Net profit}}{\text{Turnover}} \times 100$	$\dfrac{680{,}515}{7{,}103{,}495} \times 100 = 9.58\%$	(9.52%)
$\dfrac{\text{Debtors}}{\text{Turnover}} \times 365$	$\dfrac{1{,}345{,}933}{7{,}103{,}495} \times 365 = 69 \text{ days}$	(67 days)
$\dfrac{\text{Creditors}}{\text{Cost of sales}} \times 365$	$\dfrac{365{,}038}{4{,}981{,}681} \times 365 = 27 \text{ days}$	(28 days)

Conclusion: These results indicate that the financial statements are consistent within themselves. The ratios answers are as expected (indicated in planning and accounting system information) and are comparable to the previous year.

9   **Going concern**

The reasons that going concern is considered to be risky are:

1)   The audit that BCS is carrying out on its suppliers
2)   The fact that Gladys Burton is considering selling the company

Therefore, in my going concern work I would:

1) BCS

   - Enquire whether the audit has been completed and what the results were

   - Review any correspondence between BCS and Glad Rags

   - If BCS require Glad Rags to undertake certain matters, discuss with Gladys and consider whether Glad Rags is able to make the changes

   - Review the sales order book for the forthcoming period to assess whether BCS has withdrawn trade

2) Potential sale of business

   - Discuss with Gladys her plans, in particular the timescale of those plans

   - Enquire if she intends to sell the business as a going concern and the likelihood of her being able to. Review any correspondence she has had with solicitors and or valuers/estate agents

   - Review budgets for the forthcoming year for Glad Rags Limited to ensure that the company appears to still be operating as a going concern

   - Discuss with Gladys whether she has implemented succession plans within the business, given that she is a key member of staff and integral to the business

10 Management representation letter

Jules

Although in the bulk of our audit work we have not had to rely solely on representations from the director, it will still be necessary to draft a management representation letter as there are some management representations relevant to all audits.

The following matters will be covered in the letter:

1) Management's acknowledgement of its responsibility for the financial statements

2) Management's acknowledgement of its responsibility for the design and implementation of internal control systems to prevent fraud and error

3) Management's belief that the uncorrected errors listed by the auditors are in aggregate immaterial.

11 Opinion

In our opinion:

- the financial statements give a true and fair view, in accordance with United Kingdom Generally Accepted Accounting Practice, of the state of the company's affairs at 30 November 20X4 and of its profitw for the year then ended; and

- the financial statements have been properly prepared in accordance with the Companies Act 2006; and

- the information given in the Directors' Report is consistent with the financial statements.

12 a) A post balance sheet fire inspection resulting in an immaterial fine would have no effect on the audit. The financial statements would not have to be adjusted for an immaterial fine.

b) If there is no visit, then there is a potential contingent liability which should be disclosed in the financial statements. This is because the company might have to pay out some money (a fine) as a result of the non-compliance with the fire law during the year under review.

The auditors should assess the likelihood of a visit and the level of any expected fine. If they believe that it is possible that the company will have to pay a material fine in respect of the non-compliance, then they should ask the directors to disclose this contingent liability in the financial statements. If the directors refused, the auditors would be disagreeing with their treatment and would have to qualify the audit opinion on this issue.

However, if the auditors agree that the likelihood of a material fine is remote, they will not have to take any further action. They are unlikely to have a statutory duty to report the breach of law to any authority and therefore should not do so, as so doing would breach their duty of confidentiality.

13 Draft paragraph for management representation letter

In connection with the lack of disclosure for potential fines resulting from non compliance with the fire doors regulations, the directors confirm their believe that the possibility of a fine is remote, and that such a fine would be likely to be immaterial.

14 Clare is right to point out that there is an element of uncertainty existing here. However, auditors would generally only draw attention to fundamental uncertainties in their audit report, that is, uncertainties which would have a significant impact on the financial statements. It is clear that the directors firmly believe that any fine in respect of the fire doors would be immaterial and therefore it is unlikely that any outcome from this situation would have a fundamental impact on the financial statements. There is no need for the auditors to highlight this matter in their report.

15 Audit opinion

a) The director is wrong to say that the stock should be accounted for as it existed at the yearend. In fact, the problem causing the stock to be obsolete existed at the yearend and therefore the stock should be considered to be obsolete at the yearend, even if it appeared to be saleable at the stock take.

b) **Qualified opinion arising from disagreement about accounting treatment**

Included in stock in the balance sheet and the profit and loss account is an amount of £67,495 in respect of a group of plants which were damaged on the day of the stock take. In our opinion, these plants were unsaleable and therefore obsolete and should not have been included in stock, reducing profit before tax and net assets by that amount.

Except for the financial effect of the wrongful inclusion of this stock, in our opinion:

- the financial statements give a true and fair view, in accordance with United Kingdom Generally Accepted Accounting Practice, of the state of the company's affairs at 31 December 20X4 and of its profit for the year then ended; and

- the financial statements have been properly prepared in accordance with the Companies Act 2006.

- the information given in the Directors' Report is consistent with the financial statements.

PRACTICE SKILLS TEST

EGMUND LTD

ANSWERS

Task 1

Client	Egmund Ltd
Accounting date	30 September 20X7

Prepared by	A Student
Date	XX/XX/XX
Reviewed by	
Date	

a) **Control environment**

Control environment is the overall **attitude, awareness** and **actions of directors and managers** regarding internal controls and their importance in the entity. The control environment encompasses the management style, and corporate culture and values shared by all employees. It provides the background against which the various other controls are operated.

However, a strong control environment does not, by itself, ensure the effectiveness of the overall internal control system.

The following factors will be reflected in the control environment.

CONTROL ENVIRONMENT	
Philosophy and **operating style** of management	Consider attitude to controls – do management override controls? Do they neglect controls and concentrate solely on results and targets?
Organisation structure and segregation of duties	Consider delegation of authority and whether management consider competence of staff for particular jobs. Segregation of duties – the principle that no single person should record and process all stages of a transaction.
Director's methods of imposing controls	Consider extent to which management supervise operations. How do they exercise control? (budgets, management accounts and internal audit)

Segregation of duties is a vital aspect of the control environment. Segregation of duties implies a number of people being involved. Hence it is more difficult for fraudulent transactions to be processed (since a number of people would have to collude in the fraud), and it is also more difficult for accidental errors to be processed (since the more people are involved, the more checking there can be).

Smaller businesses might be able to achieve a strong control environment with less segregation of duties than a larger business. Often, in a smaller business, the directors are able to 'keep an eye' on the business without burdening it by fragmenting its organisational structure.

Most modern businesses nowadays try to be customer focused and are looking for ways to simplify and streamline their organisational structures and cut down on paperwork, so they can give customers a more efficient and speedier service.

Task 1 (continued)

Client	Egmund Ltd
Accounting date	30 September 20X7

Prepared by	A Student
Date	XX/XX/XX
Reviewed by	
Date	

b)   **Assessment of control environment**

The assessment of Egmund's control environment is STRONG

The operating style of the Hennmans is very much hands on. They keep a keen eye on what is going on and keep good links of communication with their staff, especially Shelly, the farm manager. Their teamworking approach entails a lot of openness and sharing of information which makes it difficult for staff to be perpetrating any secretive manipulation of data or fraud.

The Hennmans use their management accounts well in monitoring the performance of the business.

Shelly, the farm manager, produces statistics of daily egg production and these can be compared to both the size of the hen flock as well as actual sales turnover.

Task 2

Client	Egmund Ltd
Accounting date	30 September 20X7

Prepared by	A Student
Date	XX/XX/XX
Reviewed by	
Date	

a) **Inherent risk**

Inherent risk is the risk that items will be mis-stated due to the characteristics of those items, such as the fact that they are estimates or that they are important items in the accounts and hence there is a temptation to mis-state them. The auditors must use their professional judgement and all available knowledge to assess inherent risk. If no such information or knowledge is available then the inherent risk is high.

Where inherent risk is low, the auditors may hence assume an element of inherent assurance, thereby allowing themselves to reduce the level of assurance to be obtained from controls testing and substantive procedures.

FACTORS AFFECTING CLIENT AS A WHOLE	
Integrity and **attitude to risk** of directors and management	Domination by a single individual can cause problems
Management experience and **knowledge**	Changes in management and quality of financial management
Unusual pressures on management	Examples include tight reporting deadlines, or market or financing expectations
Nature of business	Potential problems include technological obsolescence or over-dependence on single product. Cyclical and seasonal businesses may experience periods of staff pressure which leads to errors
Industry factors	Competitive conditions, regulatory requirements, technology developments, changes in customer demand
Information technology	Problems include lack of supporting documentation, concentration of expertise in a few people, potential for unauthorised access

b) **Assessment of inherent risk**

i) **Directors and management.** There is no domination by a single individual. Teamwork is encouraged.

ii) **Management.** The Hennmans and Shelly Ovalton are well qualified for the tasks of running an egg farm.

iii) **Reporting pressures.** This is an owner-managed family business. There are no financial reporting pressures

Task 2 (continued)

Client	Egmund Ltd
Accounting date	30 September 20X7

Prepared by	A Student
Date	XX/XX/XX
Reviewed by	
Date	

iv) **Nature of business.** There are few business factors which might increase inherent risk of the entity. Very little can go wrong with eggs.

v) **Industry factors.** The industry is established and stable.

c)

FACTORS AFFECTING INHERENT RISK IN INDIVIDUAL ACCOUNT BALANCES OR TRANSACTIONS	
Financial statement **accounts prone to misstatement**	Accounts which require adjustment in previous period or require high degree of estimation
Complex accounts	Accounts which require expert valuations or are subjects of current professional discussion
Assets at risk of being **lost or stolen**	Cash, stock, portable fixed assets (computers)
Quality of **accounting systems**	Strength of individual departments (sales, purchases, cash etc)
Size of transactions	Where transactions are small in value the likelihood of material misstatement is less than where transactions are of high value
Unusual transactions	Unusual transactions, with unusual names, not settled promptly (particularly important if they occur at period-end). Transactions that do not go through the system, that relate to specific clients or processed by certain individuals.
Staff	Staff changes or areas of low morale

Task 3

Client	Egmund Ltd
Accounting date	30 September 20X7

Prepared by	A Student
Date	XX/XX/XX
Reviewed by	
Date	

a) **Sources of audit assurance**

Given per question: inherent assurance

Other sources

i) Controls assurance – from tests on internal controls

ii) Substantive assurance – from substantive tests of detail and/or substantive analytical procedures.

b) **Financial statement assertions**

i) Accuracy
ii) Completeness
iii) Cut off
iv) Classification/understandability
v) Occurence
vi) Valuation
vii) Existence
viii) Rights/obligations

c) **Test of controls**

These are tests designed to obtain sufficient appropriate audit evidence about the effective operation of the accounting and internal control systems, that is, that properly designed controls identified in preliminary assessment of control risk exist in fact and have operated effectively throughout the relevant period.

d) **Substantive procedures**

Substantive procedures are designed to confirm the **completeness**, **accuracy** and **validity** of the items in the accounts or the accounting records. Tests are also carried out to confirm that there are **no material omissions** in the accounts or accounting records. Substantive procedures will always be required even if all risks are assessed as low. They are designed to obtain evidence relating to the financial statement assertions.

Some of the financial statement assertions relate to assets and liabilities, some to transactions. In practice also some balance sheet assertions are more important for specific balance sheet items than others.

Task 3 (continued)

Client	Egmund Ltd
Accounting date	30 September 20X7

Prepared by	A Student
Date	XX/XX/XX
Reviewed by	
Date	

Substantive procedures are of two types:

i)   *Tests of detail*

These are designed to provide audit evidence about the balance or transaction and usually entail procedures such as inspection of documentation, verification of assets, confirmations from third parties and checking of calculations.

ii) *Substantive analytical procedures*

They involve the analysis of relationships:

–   Between items of financial data, or between items of financial and non-financial data, deriving from the same period, or

–   Between comparable financial information deriving from different periods to identify consistencies and predicted patterns or significant fluctuations and unexpected relationships, and the results of investigation thereof.

The key aspect to remember is that substantive analytical procedures involve the auditors developing a prediction and comparing the actual against that prediction.

For example a substantive analytical test on Egmund's sales might involve developing a prediction of eggs produced based on the number of laying hens in the flock, and the potential daily output of each laying hen based on it physical condition/age.

Task 4

Client	Egmund Ltd		Prepared by	A Student
Accounting date	30 September 20X7		Date	XX/XX/XX
			Reviewed by	
			Date	

E-MAIL MESSAGE

To: **Delsia Deans**

From: **A Student**

Subject: **Materiality**

Materiality is an expression of the relative significance or importance of a particular matter in the context of financial statements as a whole, or of individual financial statements. A matter is material if its omission or misstatement would reasonably influence the decisions of an addressee of the auditors' report.

Small amounts should be considered if there is a risk that they could occur more than once and together add up to an amount which is material in total. Also, qualitative aspects must be considered, for example the inaccurate and therefore misleading description of an accounting policy.

Materiality considerations will differ depending on the aspect of the financial statements being considered.

A good example is directors' pay, which makes normal materiality considerations irrelevant, because it must be disclosed by the auditors if is are not disclosed correctly by the directors in the financial statements.

Materiality considerations during audit planning are extremely important. The assessment of materiality when determining the nature, timing and extent of audit procedures should be based on the most recent and reliable financial information and will help to determine an effective and efficient audit approach. Materiality assessment in conjunction with risk assessment will help the auditors to make a number of decisions.

- What items to examine

- Whether to use sampling techniques

- What level of error is likely to lead to an opinion that the accounts do not give a true and fair view

The resulting combination of audit procedures should help to reduce detection risk to an appropriately low level.

Regards,

Wanda

Task 5

Client	Egmund Ltd
Accounting date	30 September 20X7

Prepared by	A Student
Date	XX/XX/XX
Reviewed by	
Date	

Debtors circularisation sample

The following balances are the largest and so have been selected.

	£
Anchor and Chain	2,413
Bakit Limited	1,125
Cakes U Like	1,275
Chopstix	1,918
Daljits Delights	1,496
Heartbreak Hotel	1,257
Honeybunn and Son	1,699
Igor Biscuits	1,835
Patel Pastries	2,475
Pie in Sky	2,109

Task 6

Client	Egmund Ltd
Accounting date	30 September 20X7

Prepared by	A Student
Date	XX/XX/XX
Reviewed by	
Date	

Debtors circularisation

Objective

To confirm the existence, recording accuracy and valuation of sales ledger balances.

Work done

Confirmation requests were sent to a sample of 10 debtors.

Results

The following replies were received:

Customer	Balance per Egmund Ltd	Balance per reply	Reconciling items
Anchor and Chain	2,413	1,963	Cheque received on 2/10 – £450
Bakit Ltd	1,125	1,075	Goods returned – £50 – agreed to credit note reserve.
Chopstix	1,918	1,798	Disputed invoice No. 4848 – £120 – agreed to bad debt provision
Honeybunn and Son	1,699	1,663	Invoice 492 incorrectly processed by Egmund as £51 instead of £15
Igor Biscuits	1,835	1,835	–
Pie in Sky	2,109	1,784	Cheque received on 6/10 – £325

There is therefore a potential adjustment of a reduction in debtors of £36 relating to Honeybunn and Son. All other amounts either agreed or were satisfactorily reconciled.

Conclusion

Alternative procedures must be carried out on the balances for which no reply has been received before a conclusion can be reached. These may include testing to cash received after date, or where this is not possible, the balance should be analysed and agreed to the sales invoice and delivery notes signed by customers acknowledging receipt of delivery.

Task 7

Client	Egmund Ltd
Accounting date	30 September 20X7

Prepared by	A Student
Date	XX/XX/XX
Reviewed by	
Date	

Stage	Control objectives	Controls
1 Order	All orders are genuinely for business use and authorised	Central policy for choosing suppliers Pre-numbered order forms Safeguarding of blank order forms Authorisation of order
2 Goods received	Goods are as were ordered Goods received are recorded	Inspection of goods received Goods received notes Checking goods received notes to orders Signatures to evidence checking done
3 Invoice	Liabilities are only recognised for goods and services that have been received Invoices are recorded	Invoices are checked to goods received notes Calculations on supplier's invoices checked Referencing of supplier's invoices Correct classification of invoice (expense or asset) Signatures evidencing checking performed
4 Payment	The company only pays genuine business expenses	Cheque requisition supported by payment documentation (eg invoices) Cheques signed by two authorised personnel Prompt despatch of cheques Payment documentation cancelled when paid

Task 8

Client	Egmund Ltd
Accounting date	30 September 20X7

Prepared by	A Student
Date	XX/XX/XX
Reviewed by	
Date	

Internal control weaknesses in purchases and payments system

1 Orders made out by the farm manageress are not independently authorised by another person.

2 There is a lack of separation between the person ordering goods and the person confirming due receipt on behalf of the company. The farm manageress carries out both responsibilities.

3 The delivery note is not signed in evidence of the checking that has been done.

4 Farm assistants may be involved in receiving and checking deliveries to the company.

5 There appears to be no checking of prices and calculations shown on suppliers invoices.

6 The farm manager is able to order goods as well as approve them for payment. These responsibilities should be separated.

7 There are no procedures to establish the liabilities in respect of deliveries received but not yet invoiced, ie listing of outstanding delivery notes in file kept in barn.

8 Cheques should ideally be signed by two people.

Task 9

Client	Egmund Ltd
Accounting date	30 September 20X7

Prepared by	A Student
Date	XX/XX/XX
Reviewed by	
Date	

Purchases and payments

Substantive tests of detail

a) Trace invoice to order form to ensure that the items have been properly ordered.

b) Check quantities to delivery note to confirm that goods received were as invoiced. Ensure that box is signed by farm manager Shelly Ovalton,

c) Verify that invoices are approved by the appropriate people: Shelly Ovalton; Joyti Hennman or Harry Hennman.

d) Ensure correct cheque number and date are recorded on the invoice.

e) Check casts and extensions on invoice

f) Confirm correct prices have been charged either by reference to an approved price list or by discussion with Joyti or Harry Hennman.

g) Trace posting to correct account in nominal ledger.

Task 10

Client	Egmund Ltd
Accounting date	30 September 20X7

Prepared by	A Student
Date	XX/XX/XX
Reviewed by	
Date	

Identifying year-end creditors

Outstanding unpaid invoices can be identified by going to the Unpaid Invoices file.

However, the company must also pick up the liability for goods received at the farm but not yet invoiced by suppliers as at the year-end.

Therefore, the company must also prepare and evaluate a list of creditors from the file, kept in the barn, of delivery notes pending receipt of suppliers' invoices.

Task 11

Client	Egmund Ltd
Accounting date	30 September 20X7

Prepared by	A Student
Date	XX/XX/XX
Reviewed by	
Date	

Stocks of eggs and fresh chickens

a) No this does not constitute a lack of proper accounting records because the farm does not usually have material stocks of eggs or fresh chickens at the end of a day.

In practice, many smaller companies will ascertain closing stocks by conducting a physical count at year-end.

b) The level of control to be exercised over the eggs and chickens will be influenced by their susceptability to theft/misappropriation. This appears to be low because of the low value of eggs, their fragility and short useful life. Similarly, it would be difficult to hide a chicken under ones clothes and walk out of the farm.

The team working and open plan nature of the working environment also militates against an employee being able to get away with any misappropriation as it would have to be committed within the gaze of colleagues.

c) i) Obtain the farm manager's charts for the year showing egg production.

ii) Review figures shown on chart against size of flock and laying capacity of the hens. Take into consideration any factors that might impact on productivity.

iii) Select four weeks, spread through the year, and track sales of eggs invoiced against eggs produced.

iv) Work out total eggs produced during the financial year, evaluate this at an average selling price and compare it to actual egg sales for the year.

d) Our audit enquires revealed that there were no detailed records of eggs produced or records to control stock movements of eggs and fresh chickens. We appreciate that it is difficult to misappropriate stocks of eggs and that the directors exercise top-down control over the number of eggs produced and eggs sold, on a quarterly basis through a management reporting system.

Our recommendation is, therefore, that the directors might consider the benefits of establishing detailed stock records to strengthen the control over egg production and movement of stocks on a day-to-day basis.

Task 12

Client	Egmund Ltd
Accounting date	30 September 20X7

Prepared by	A Student
Date	XX/XX/XX
Reviewed by	
Date	

Payroll system control objectives

1) Employees are only paid for work done.
2) The correct employees are paid.
3) Deductions are calculated correctly and authorised.

Task 13

Client	Egmund Ltd
Accounting date	30 September 20X7

Prepared by	A Student
Date	XX/XX/XX
Reviewed by	
Date	

Audit report opinion paragraph

The appropriate opinion paragraph would be set out as follows:

Qualified opinion arising from disagreement about accounting treatment

Included in debtors shown in the balance sheet is an amount of £2,475 which is unlikely to be recovered. Egmund Ltd has no security for this debt. In our opinion full provision of £2,475 should have been made, reducing profit before tax and net assets by that amount.

Except for the financial effect of the absence of this provision, in our opinion:

- the financial statements give a true and fair view, in accordance with United Kingdom Generally Accepted Accounting Practice, of the state of the company's affairs as at 30 September 20X7 and of its profit for the year then ended; and

- the financial statements have been properly prepared in accordance with the Companies Act 2006; and

- the information given in the Directors' Report is consistent with the financial statements.

A Byrdez
Registered auditors   30 September 20X7

Task 14

Client	Egmund Ltd
Accounting date	30 September 20X7

Prepared by	A Student
Date	XX/XX/XX
Reviewed by	
Date	

MEMO

To: Delsia Deans

From: A Student

Date: XX/XX/XX

Subject: Confidentiality and safe custody of working papers

I am writing to you to reiterate our responsibilities for the safe custody of our working papers and the confidential nature of the information we are working with.

Auditors should adopt appropriate procedures for maintaining the confidentiality and safe custody of their working papers.

When we are working on site and we leave our desk to go to lunch, or at the end of the day, we should always clear away our work and keep it in a safe place where it cannot be seen by unauthorised people. The payroll contains very sensitive information so this is particularly important for wages work.

All information that we obtain during the course of an audit should be treated as confidential and not shared with anyone outside our firm. So when we take work home with us we must not allow anyone access to our files, or lose the files.

AAT SPECIMEN SKILLS TEST

ANSWERS

ANSWERS (Task 1)

Client	DJs Ltd
Accounting date	31/12/02

Prepared by	A Student
Date	xx/xx/xx
Reviewed by	
Date	

Sales

The business deals in a lot of cash sales which means there is scope for theft and understatement of sales. It is therefore a high risk area in this audit.

Purchases and creditors

These are likely to be one of the most material areas of the audit. Purchases will be made frequently and so there is likely to be a high number of transactions giving scope for error. The creditors figure is likely to be one of the most significant figures on the balance sheet (especially since there will be no trade debtors), and will have the same inherent risks as purchases.

Payroll

The seasonal nature of the business means there are likely to be large numbers of staff coming and going. This leads to risks of incorrect deductions being made and failure to comply with the pay as you earn rules.

Fixed assets

This is likely to be a material figure on the balance sheet, and incorrect analysis could lead to distortion of the profit and loss account.

22

ANSWERS (Task 2)

Client	DJs Ltd
Accounting date	31/12/02

Prepared by	A Student
Date	xx/xx/xx
Reviewed by	
Date	

Weakness	Error or irregularity
There is no password protection for the computer, and staff are allowed into the office unsupervised.	It would be possible for staff to access the payroll programme and change their rates of pay, which may go unnoticed. Staff could have access to confidential financial information about the business.
There is little follow up to differences between the takings in the till and the takings per the till roll. Also daily takings are totalled by one of the managers, both of whom have only recently been employed.	Although the individual differences may be small this could lead to a significant loss of money over a period, and could be as a result of theft. In addition, the business is paying VAT on takings that have not actually been received. It may not be sensible to assume that the managers are trustworthy.
There is a lack of discipline over accounting for the cash taken for expenses from the tills.	If staff are aware that money can be taken from the tills without the need to account for it they may take the opportunity to take money for themselves.
Cash is kept on the premises.	High risk of theft.
The head chef is responsible for making the purchase orders and also for checking the deliveries.	This lack of segregation of duties gives the opportunity to order goods which are not required and to keep them. There is also the opportunity for a 'kick back' system, where the amount recorded on the invoice is for more than was actually received and the difference is split between the supplier and the chef.

23

ANSWERS (Task 2, continued)

Client	DJs Ltd
Accounting date	31/12/02

Prepared by	A Student
Date	xx/xx/xx
Reviewed by	
Date	

Weakness	Error or irregularity
There is no check from the invoice to the delivery note before it is paid.	The invoice may be made out for goods that were not received, so resulting in overpayment of purchases.
The bookkeeper is responsible for calculating the wages and for paying them out.	This gives the bookkeeper a great deal of control over cash and there is scope for direct theft, or for deliberately overstating the wages of staff with whom the bookkeeper may be in league.
The staff are responsible for recording their own hours of work, and there is no check on this.	It is possible for staff to overstate the hours they worked. Even if this was only a small amount each week, it could mount up to a significant overstatement over time.
Only four required.	

24

ANSWERS (Task 3)

Client	DJs Ltd
Accounting date	31/12/02

Prepared by	A Student
Date	xx/xx/xx
Reviewed by	
Date	

Audit objectives:
All sales are recorded.
Sales have been recorded accurately.

Tests of control

Observation tests to see that all sales are being entered into the till when they are made.

Review of comparisons between till rolls and takings sheets to see that this is being done even though only large amounts are followed through.

Test of details

Check totals from till roll to takings sheets.

Check from takings sheets to bank statements.

Check that totals on the takings sheets are properly entered into the accounts.

Analytical procedures

Compare sales by month to the preceding years.

Compare sales to purchases via the gross profit percentage.

Compare expenses to sales to ensure they are an appropriate proportion.

25

ANSWERS (Task 3, continued)

Client	DJs Ltd
Accounting date	31/12/02

Prepared by	A Student
Date	xx/xx/xx
Reviewed by	
Date	

Limitations of audit evidence

Tests of control

Observation tests may give a false idea of how things are actually being done as people tend to behave differently when they know they are being observed.

In a situation like this where there are few controls in operation there is not a lot of point in testing controls which are known to be weak as it will not add to the audit evidence, but simply confirm the need to do more detailed testing.

The sample may be biased and may not reflect the characteristics of the population.

Test of details

The tests can only test what has actually been recorded, so if a sale has been made but not recorded the tests will not pick this up.

The sample may be biased and may not reflect the characteristics of the population.

Analytical procedures

In a business like this it is difficult to make accurate predictions, and whilst trends can be predicted it would be very difficult to gain any reassurance from a comparison with previous years.

Comparing sales to purchases can give good evidence, but only if the auditor is sure that the purchases figure is correct. There is a danger of proving sales by looking at purchases and vice versa and not confirming either of them by other means.

26

ANSWERS (Task 4)

Client	DJs Ltd
Accounting date	31/12/02

Prepared by	A Student
Date	xx/xx/xx
Reviewed by	
Date	

i) Factors to take into account when determining the sample size for creditors:

- the number of items in the population;
- the likelihood of error;
- the amount of evidence obtained by other means i.e. analytical procedures and tests of control;
- the value of individual items;
- the materiality of the balance;
- the tolerable error.

ii) When testing for understatement the auditor should start with the source of the transaction. In the case of creditors this would be the purchase order. However the purchase orders from throughout the year are unlikely still to be with the creditors, so it is advisable to select the creditors with the most activity during the year (this is not necessarily those with the largest balance at the year end), as they have the most opportunity for errors to occur.

27

ANSWERS (Task 5)

Client	DJs Ltd
Accounting date	31/12/02

Prepared by	A Student
Date	xx/xx/xx
Reviewed by	
Date	

Purchases review points

1. The working paper has not been properly headed up with the company name and who prepared it.

2. The test is to ensure that purchases are not overstated, and therefore the starting point for the sample should be the nominal ledger and not the purchase invoice.

3. The sample size was supposed to be 15 according to the planning, and only 12 have been tested.

4. Items 1 to 4 have purchase invoice numbers which look very close together given that the sample should have been selected on a systematic basis.

5. Item 4: the description is 'dog food' which does not look like a business expense.

6. Item 9 has been marked as 'not found'. This is an error which should be followed up; it is not sufficient simply to replace it with another invoice.

7. A Christmas advert should not be included in purchases.

8. The conclusion is not valid given the above points.

28

ANSWERS (Task 6)

Client	DJs Ltd
Accounting date	31/12/02

Prepared by	A Student
Date	xx/xx/xx
Reviewed by	
Date	

Creditors statement reconciliation

Creditor	Balance per client (£)	Balance per statement (£)	Agrees to statement	Reconciled
Boozers	4,069.56	5,971.42		✓
Jo Bakers	425.35	425.35	✓	
Coffee Club	1,287.10	Not available		
Foodies	3,924.50	3,924.50	✓	
Heatons	1,008.18	Not available		
The Meat Club	2,478.64	2,478.64	✓	
Olivers Ltd	1,036.50	973.50		✓
The Veg Shop	210.10	220.34		✓

Objectives

To ensure that creditors are correctly stated.

Reconciliations

Boozers

	£
Balance per client	4,069.56
Cash in transit	1,817.16
Invoice in transit	84.70
Balance per statement	5,971.42

Olivers Ltd

	£
Balance per client	1,036.50
Input error inv. 31534 £281 instead of £218	(63.00)
	973.50

29

ANSWERS (Task 6, continued)

Client	DJs Ltd		Prepared by	A Student
Accounting date	31/12/02		Date	xx/xx/xx
			Reviewed by	
			Date	

The Veg Shop

	£
Balance per client	210.10
Credit note not on statement	10.24
Balance per statement	220.34

Additional work

It will be necessary to follow up the items on each of the reconciliations to ensure they are valid. The invoice and credit note should be agreed to the actual documents, and the cash in transit should be agreed to the bank payments.

The two balances for whom there was no statement should be verified by other means. This could include agreeing the balance to the individual purchase invoices, and also reviewing after date invoices to ensure that there are none which relate to the year ended 31 December 2002.

30

ANSWERS (Task 7)

Client	
Accounting date	

Prepared by	
Date	
Reviewed by	
Date	

Fixed assets: review of repairs and renewals

	£	Transfer to fixed assets
Replacement Plates	1,670	✓
Maintenance of tills	400	
Computer software	150	
New chairs for outside	2,500	✓
Paper napkins	357	
Repair of fridge	125	
Coffee making machine	4,500	✓
Decorator: wall papering restaurant	500	
Annual maintenance of security system	200	
Grass cutting: weekly	500	
Repair of dishwasher	97	
Replacement dishwasher	980	✓
Picture hanging	125	
Mural painted on restaurant wall	900	
Plant care	3,000	
New cutlery	5,000	✓
Tea towels	200	
Sign writing for outside	350	

31

ANSWERS (Task 7, continued)

Client	DJs Ltd
Accounting date	31/12/02

Prepared by	A Student
Date	xx/xx/xx
Reviewed by	
Date	

Tests to confirm that fixed assets are complete and that they exist

Perform a physical verification, testing from assets recorded to the physical asset, and testing from the assets in the restaurant to ensure they are recorded.

Test to confirm that fixed assets are accurately recorded

Agree the fixed asset to the invoice, checking that the amount and classification are correct and that the invoice is made out to the company.

32

ANSWERS (Task 8)

Client	DJs Ltd
Accounting date	31/12/02

Prepared by	A Student
Date	xx/xx/xx
Reviewed by	
Date	

All matters relating to the audit are confidential and should not be discussed with anyone other than those directly involved with the audit.

This should be explained to the friend, and if she does not accept it, it would be advisable not to meet up with her during the time of the audit.

It would also be advisable to explain the situation to the audit partner.

33

ANSWERS (Task 9)

Client	DJs Ltd
Accounting date	31/12/02

Prepared by	A Student
Date	xx/xx/xx
Reviewed by	
Date	

Objective: to ensure money is not lost through theft or fraud.

Current situation	Recommendation for improvement
The computer is accessible to all and there is is no password protection.	It is recommended that a password is created for the computer and only made known to authorised personnel. It would be advisable to have a lock on the office door if this is practical.
Where there is a lot of cash there will always be the possibility of theft, but the lack of discipline over the cash expenses and the failure to follow up differences between the till rolls and the cash in the till increase the risk of theft going unnoticed. It is also a risk to allow one person to cash up at the end of the day.	A petty cash system should be in operation so that it is unnecessary to use money from the till. Any differences between the till roll and the cash in the till will therefore have to be down to error or theft. It is recognised that to check every difference is impractical, but a running total of the differences should be maintained so that the total effect can be monitored. It is advisable to have two people cashing up as it reduces the opportunity for theft.
The head chef is responsible for making the orders and also for checking them in. This gives the opportunity for fraud as there is no other person to check the delivery to the order.	It is recommended that another person is involved in the process, preferably one of the managers, so that there is an independent check on the goods received to the order.
Staff record their own hours which may lead to overstatement of hours worked.	It is recommended that a manager monitors the hours worked and checks that the hours recorded are accurate.

34

ANSWERS (Task 9, continued)

Client	DJs Ltd
Accounting date	31/12/02

Prepared by	A Student
Date	xx/xx/xx
Reviewed by	
Date	

Objective: to ensure money is not lost through theft or fraud.

Current situation	Recommendation for improvement
The bookkeeper has access to cash and there is no check on the wages paid out. This could result in overpayment of staff or theft by the bookkeeper.	It is recommended that one of the owners or both of the managers count the cash into the pay envelope. It is also recommended that the payroll is reviewed by the managers or owners before the employees are paid to ensure there is nothing unusual.
Only four required.	

35

ANSWERS (Task 10)

Client	DJs Ltd
Accounting date	31/12/X2

Prepared by	A Student
Date	xx/xx/xx
Reviewed by	
Date	

i) The audit opinion should be qualified on the grounds of limitation of scope. Since it will not render the accounts misleading the qualification should be 'except for'.

ii) The opinion paragraph would be as follows:

Qualified opinion arising from limitation in audit scope

Except for the financial effects of any adjustments that might have been found to be necessary had we been able to obtain sufficient audit evidence concerning cash sales, in our opinion:

- the financial statements give a true and fair view in accordance with United Kingdom Generally Accepted Accounting Practice, of the state of the company's affairs as at 31 December 20X2 and of its profit for the year then ended;

- the financial statements have been properly prepared in accordance with the Companies Act 2006; and

- the information given in the Directors' Report is consistent with the financial statements.

In respect alone of the limitation on our work relating to cash sales:

- we have not obtained all the information and explanations that we considered necessary for the purpose of our audit; and

- we were unable to determine whether proper accounting records had been maintained.

36